We have heard the last sad lullaby and prayer for a dead child:

> Go to thy rest, fair child,
> Go to thy dreamless bed,
> While yet so young and undefiled,
> With blessings on thy head.

and the sound of grief as natural, heartbroken conversation in this tribute to Mike who died in 1919:

> His gentle, young life was one of extreme
> Kindness and affection to Mama, Papa, and Friends.
> He did his best to make us happy and proud of him.

We have sorrowed for John Richard Wiggins:

> The youth hath died in a strange land.

and followed Thomas and Rebecca Williams in three long processions to offer up the bodies of their infants:

> We lay our children in the tomb,
> In faith their spirits at thy feet we see.

⇒ GONE HOME ⇐

and looked hard at the stone covering little Mollie Russell who lived only twelve days:

> A little time on earth she spent.

Again and again, we hear Mariah Ann Shepherd calling to her children:

> Rise, children, rise from the encumbrance of clay;
> Give heed to my call, Come away, Come away.

Often we breathed the air of a young state and land, as at the grave of Colonel Charles McLemore, a member of the General Assembly of Alabama:

> He was gifted and brilliant, gentle but knightly,
> and no truer patriot sleeps beneath the sod of Alabama.

We tipped a hat to

> John Ellis McNeill, 46th Ala, Fought in 27 Battles,
> Unscratched, Died in 1867

We yearned to speak with Araminta E. Collins, 1858-1911:

> The law of truth was in her mouth. And she walked
> with God in peace.

But no gravestone writing has ever moved us as this one from an unlettered hand and noble heart:

> Preshers Memerey
> Glorey to God

Fig. 1: Commemorative marble arch leading to a family grave site.

GONE HOME

SOUTHERN FOLK GRAVESTONE ART

Compiled and edited by

Jack and Olivia Solomon

Photographs by

Suzannah Solomon

NEWSOUTH BOOKS

Montgomery

NewSouth Books
P.O. Box 1588
Montgomery, AL 36102

Library of Congress Cataloging-in-Publication Data

Solomon, Jack, and Solomon, Olivia,
Gone home / by Jack Solomon and Olivia Solomon.
p.   cm.
ISBN 1-58838-116-1
1. Alabama—Social life and customs. 2. Epitaphs—Alabama. 3. Burial—Alabama. 4.
Folk art—Alabama—Themes, motives. 5. Folklore—Alabama. I. Solomon, Jack, 1927- ,
Solomon, Olivia, 1937- . II. Title.

F330.S66 1996   93-8598
929'.5'09761—dc20   CIP

Printed in the United States of America.

Designed by Randall Williams
Cover designed by Rhonda Reynolds

To the Glory of God
And in Memory of Our Parents

Mackie Hornsby Pienezza

May 24, 1912

May 11, 1993

Lucy Hill Payne Solomon

November 26, 1905

April 4, 1992

Harry Merrill Pienezza

October 16, 1910

August 28, 1953

Marion Hix Solomon

April 22, 1895

Sept. 6, 1966

And the Elmore County Attorney

J. W. Pienezza

April 16, 1915

July 29, 1990

CONTENTS

Acknowledgments

Friends, relatives, neighbors, students, colleagues, grave diggers, undertakers, preachers, and innumerable other folks have all contributed to this book. We are especially grateful to the staff of the Thomas D. Russell Library of Central Alabama Community College in Alexander City, Alabama: Carolyn Ingram, Joyce Robinson, and Frances Tapley were patient and persistent in their efforts to locate materials necessary to our research.

The initial collection of epitaphs was gathered by Troy State University students enrolled in an introductory folklore course, 1958-1962, from rural and small town cemeteries in southeastern Alabama, principally in the counties of Pike, Coffee, Crenshaw, Monroe, Montgomery, Butler, Bullock, Dale, Escambia, Covington, and Lowndes. For over two decades, we have conducted field studies in numerous cemeteries throughout Lee, Elmore, Tallapoosa, Macon, Coosa, Montgomery, Autauga, Chambers, Wilcox, Sumter, Baldwin, Perry, Talladega, and Dallas counties.

The photographs were taken in many different locations across south Alabama, among them Emmaus Cemetery in Luverne, Providence and Damascus Cemeteries in Crenshaw County, Elam Primitive Baptist Church Cemetery in Pike County, Auburn Cemetery in Auburn, Tuskegee Cemetery in Tuskegee, Marion Cemetery in Marion, Greenwood Cemetery in Montgomery, Live Oak Cemetery in Selma, Livingston Cemetery in Livingston, Wetumpka Cemetery in Wetumpka, Westview Cemetery in LaFayette, and Church Street Cemetery in Mobile. Our gratitude is extended to those who tend these cemeteries.

We thank the living and we thank those who came before us for this rich legacy of remembrance.

PREFACE

*G*one Home contains a hundred or so epitaphs out of the seven hundred edited and culled from thousands collected over four decades. Our graveyard visitations have been a constant in our lives. During our courtship and the early years of our marriage we accompanied Troy State University students on field trips in southeast Alabama, and began the practice of stopping willy-nilly at this cemetery and that on short excursions. The original intent was simply to gather inscriptions, but soon we began to notice different styles in monuments, lettering, and carving and recurrent imagery, symbolism, and themes.

By 1975 we had three children and always took them along. Our younger daughter, Suzannah, was interested in photography, and one day, unbidden, she brought her camera—the photographs in this volume follow her progress from her sixth-grade Instamatic efforts through increasingly complex cameras and lenses. Jacqueline, the elder, a furiously fast recorder, invariably gravitated to the unusual, and recognized variants immediately. Over the years, she made many helpful suggestions about the arrangement and presentation of this volume. Will, the youngest, brushed off moss, vines, and lichen, and by second grade was reading inscriptions from parts of the stone not easily accessible to grown-ups and taking rubbings on butcher paper.

As family recreation, this sort of research wasn't, at first, too popular—nobody else's Mama and Papa always picnicked near an old cemetery. Gradually, though, our small journeys were transformed into pilgrimages, undertaken in every season—under the hard, deep blue of a frozen January sky, in the days of new green and vistas of wild roses and honeysuckle, in the dry August crackle of locusts, and in that remarkable October light which so brilliantly shows forth the scarlet and gold dying. And the seasons of earth are like the seasons of man: they teach us not to fear.

Sometimes we met mourners come with tribute. Once we encountered a venerable gravedigger, and once as we stood before the graves of a sister and brother who died the same day, an elder of the community told us their story. They lived right there, top of the hill. Their mother washed all that summer day and her children played in the woods and meadow nearby, nibbling all those hours on poisonous fruit which they mistook for wild strawberries, and by nightfall they were dead.

Always, those we met knew another cemetery we should visit. And so we'd go there and find more carvings, stories, and mourners. In Tallapoosa County a few miles from Dadeville, lovely Red Ridge Methodist Church, well over a century old, nestles against a steep hill. There, nine infants, born in nine consecutive years, lie in a row beside their mother and father. Not far is Agricola where rests a plantation owner's son murdered by a servant. In every cemetery we have been humbled again and again by the acute consciousness not of mortality but of our brotherhood with all men, and, despite our most rigid intellectual control, we have sorrowed and wept. With Othello we have murmured, "O, the pity of it, Iago, O, the pity of it." One exquisite autumn day in a rural Crenshaw County cemetery we came upon a beautiful, small marble slab on which were carved a simple cross and the words: "Walk softly, our son sleeps here." So perfect a symbol of child and father and mother, of love and remembrance, was this little monument that for many weeks we did not, could not, seek out any other.

   Gone Home is for the beauty of the earth, the time of man, for the timeless earth, for the beauty and timelessness of man, of the generations of man:

   Gone, and the seasons that come and go
   And wreath the grave in blossom and snow.

Fig. 3: Emmaus cemetery, Luverne, Alabama.

INTRODUCTION

This book is a collection of gravestone inscriptions gathered from cemeteries in central and southeast Alabama. The study of memorial art and literature began with late eighteenth century English and European antiquarians. It now encompasses the investigation of all folk phenomena associated with death and dying: customs, beliefs, superstitions, rites and practices, and ceremonies; vernacular literature extant in stone, print, and oral tradition; folk monumental architecture and sculpture, especially their ornament and symbol; and peripheral narrative and musical lore. All these expressions are interconnected, and an ideal study would present findings from history, archaeology, the arts, psychosocial sciences, and folklore. The editors, however, are not specialists, but rather lovers of the folk, and we intend to present these Alabama epitaphs as expressions of the American character, for in these writings the folk speak their minds and hearts. Puritan preachers recommended the graveyard for its terrible didactic power, as a gruesome reminder of ravaging Death, Sin, and Time, and to this day, the sensibility may be so aroused. But kinder, gentler feelings also may be stirred by leisurely hours spent in a burying ground. Over the years of recording inscriptions, there came to us gradually an indescribable satisfaction, the discovery of our fellow men congregated on a piece of earth we still, rightly, call holy.

Cemeteries run the gamut of human personality and experience: forlorn, isolated, shabby, modest, respectable, luxurious, eccentric, proud, ostentatious. They offer historic, social, and economic commentary, and the profile of an entire town may be laid bare in a glimpse: in the center, enclosed by an ornately wrought fence, rest the founding families beneath great oaks, cedars, and magnolias; nearby loom marbles and granites of an emerging mercantile or professional class, a giant obelisk raised to a distinguished son or patriot, a plain, solid stone erected to a loved preacher or teacher; and stretching out in all directions the stones of ordinary folk. About these last there is a sweet sameness, broken now and then by a brooding angel, a great arch or cross, a lovely maiden, a charming child, or a simple mausoleum, though more often, by subtle gradations in height, curve, and line. The eye and heart are comforted by these simple stones, for they resemble nothing so much as beds, cradles, and tables, the commonest furniture of earthly existence. Paradoxically, these burying grounds show far more of folk life than of death. Here may be encountered all mortal qualities: wit, passion, bravery, endurance, affection, loyalty, innocence, grace, beauty, thrift, brilliance, industry, hate, cowardice, arrogance, and here we meet again husbands and fathers, wives and mothers, children, kinsmen, neighbors, enemies, and friends.

This book is, if you will, a Platonic graveyard which mirrors cemeteries in towns, cities, and rural areas throughout Alabama from c. 1780 to 1960. Our findings over the last twenty-five years bear out what we early suspected: the same epitaphs appear again and again in different cemeteries, and one might as well be in Marion as Auburn, Mt. Gilead as Shiloh. But not quite. Each graveyard is a community with its own history and with clear reflections of state, regional, and national history. More important is personal history, the record, however brief, of a single individual who lived and died in a particular time and place. This juxtaposition of community, of a deeply shared folk continuum, of universal human attributes, with the endless variety of man as a separate being is a distinguishing characteristic of all folklore. Such an odd simultaneity is a hallmark of epitaphs, which, except for those biographical inscriptions specific to an individual, are fundamentally anonymous, held in common by Anglo-American folk for over three hundred years, a body of traditional poetry and prose, language, symbol, image, and metaphor transmitted, like all lore of the folk, over time and space, changing, yet remaining the same. Although some may be attributed to definite sources—Shakespeare, the Bible, and hymns among the most common—and although a few were composed by contemporary authors, the extractions have long since passed over into folk domain, and the individual writings, even when pseudo-literary, belong, in the main, to the folk.

Early collectors of Anglo-American epitaphs doted on the quaint, humorous, and morbid. Regrettably, that attitude persists in the general public and in some contemporary anthologists. The popular appeal of the epitaph as entertainment may be rooted in our helplessness before the mystery of death. We exorcise our fears by finding comedy where none was ever intended, mock images of disease, grin snidely at hints of venal sins, and ridicule the bombast, rhetoric, and sentimentality of gravestone writings. Save for occasional crude humor and Halloween, the epitaph is thoroughly out of fashion, and the ancient cemetery is often regarded as a sideshow of horrors, freaks, primitive beliefs, and ignorant superstitions. Our studies do not support such a view. For example, the infamous whiskey-bottle tomb of the fabulous drunkard in Clayton, Alabama, which has provoked so much comment, scholarly and otherwise, is not, after all, a replica of the liquor bottle which is reported to have killed the poor fellow, but only a larger version of a "bottle" tombstone shape common in Anglo-American folk burial architecture. Similarly, these vernacular gravestone writings are specimens of folk literature animated by the very highest human instincts and feelings. Their syntax, vocabulary, metaphors, symbols, images and poetic devices are folk derivations of English and American lyric, dramatic, and narrative genres infused with the speech of pew and pulpit, of the courthouse, town square, and marketplace, of front porch and fire place. Something, though, there must be which binds us to the epitaph, perhaps some half-remembered respect for its substance and some

Fig. 4, above left: Woodmen of the World monument: mutilated Tree of Life bearing scroll and emblem. Fig. 5, above right: Babe sleeping against the Blasted Tree. Fig. 6, below: Sleeping marble child with nosegay.

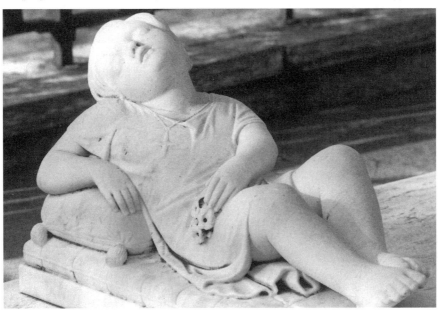

Fig. 7, above left: Tomb of the folk "drunkard" in Clayton, Alabama; the bottle shape is actually fairly common.
Fig. 8, below left: Book monument suggests both the Holy Bible and the Book of Life wherein are inscribed the names of the immortal; the inscription appears on the front cover and the architectural column serves as the spine.
Fig. 9, above right: Obelisk with carved urn; the base is carved in four headstone shapes suitable for inscription.
Fig. 10, below: Latin cross affixed to base of several architectural designs, with recessed circular crucifix and scrolls.

pleasure in its form, and surely our whimsical fondness compels us to an intelligent appreciation of this vibrant folk phenomenon.

Except for isolated instances, the gradual disappearance of the epitaph was mostly complete by 1950. To document its decline and death, together with the corollary in cemetery sculpture, architecture, decoration, and iconography, is to raise some important questions about modern man in the Western world. As early as 1890, English memorial artists, reformers, and scholars were repudiating Gothic fantasy, Romantic sensibility, and Victorian excess, and calling for a simpler, "dignified" Roman style. Much of their effort was to the good. Church graveyards, rural and urban, were sometimes little more than charnel houses, and the advocacy of large municipal cemeteries resulted in the establishment, throughout England and America, of memorial parks and gardens which displayed a richly diverse aesthetic. Today, row on row of the dead lie under the look-alike stones, carved with only a name and a birth and death date. Though it is pointless to lament or praise this homogeneity, the folklorist will wish to discover its causes. An explanation of sorts lies at hand in the triumph of technology and democracy. Mass production displaced thousands of traditional craftsmen, among them gravestone carvers who might expend months to ornament, sculpt, and inscribe a single stone. The machine item could be replicated quickly, cheaply, and endlessly, like the "store bought" dress or suit, and most people could afford a memorial as good as the next fellow's. While the contemporary cemetery may not be so interesting as those of the eighteenth and nineteenth centuries, the ideals of equality and liberty may be better served. Curiously, the stones of 2000 are reminiscent of the very earliest Anglo-European grave memorials, simple, direct, and poignant in their reminder of our common humanity.

Though it appears that folk burial arts now exist only as relics of the past, folk lore and life do not suddenly vanish; instead, they evolve organically, translated into different and new expressive media. Even if the epitaph has ceased to be a prevailing folk genre, its language, symbolism, and logical and figurative content endure under other guises: the inscription which details a long, painful illness of the deceased has become the folk narrative of our own twentieth century plagues, cancer and AIDS, a litany recited daily by horrified witnesses and piteous victims; the rhetoric of the patriot's epitaph resounds in the chambers of state legislatures and the United States Congress; the corruptibility of flesh and this world and the incorruptibility of eternity are shouted and chanted in the sermons of media evangelists seven days a week; late night television and the cinema feast on necrological images, sentimental verses appear on countless greeting cards, and the sentimental tear is shed every soap-opera afternoon in America. Similarly, tombstone decorations, ornaments, emblems, and icons appear in contemporary crafts, especially the geometric, botanical, and zoological motifs of embroidery, quilting, crochet, and woodworking; and graphic design, calligraphic arts, and hand-produced books draw on the traditions of folk gravestone carvings. In short, vernacular gravestone traditions still flourish save on the stones we erect to our dead.

In the context of galactic time, all memorials are futile. The inscription on the colossus in Shelley's poem "Ozymandias" reads: "Look on my works, ye mighty, and despair." And Washington Irving wrote in "Westminster Abbey":

> History fades into fable, fact becomes clouded with doubt and controversy, the inscription moulders from the tablet, the statue falls from the pedestal. Columns, arches, pyramids—what are they but heaps of sand? And their epitaphs, but characters written in the dust? . . . Thus man passes away; his name perishes from record and recollection; his history is as a tale that is told, and his very monument becomes a ruin. *

Often we have pondered the practical extinction of the epitaph and the general interest it still commands, but on one occasion we were astonished at the tenacious strength of its language. An Elmore County, Alabama, attorney, having learned of our interest in graveyards, described the mausoleum of a certain prominent family whose legendary history he then vividly recounted: "For all the sons were gallant, and all the daughters beautiful." Much later, we came upon the following epitaph which Irving appended to "Westminster Abbey" **

> Here lyes the Loyal Duke of Newcastle, and his Duchess, his second wife, by whom he had no issue. Her name was Margaret Lucas, youngest sister to the Lord Lucas of Colchester, a noble family; for all the brothers were valiant, and all the sisters virtuous. This Duchess was a wise, witty, and learned lady, which her many Bookes do well testify; she was a most virtuous, and loving and careful wife, and was with her lord all the time of his banishment and miseries, and when he came home, never parted from him in his solitary retirement. . . . I do not know an epitaph that breathes a loftier consciousness of family worth and honorable lineage than one which affirms of a noble house that "all the brothers were brave and all the sisters virtuous." ***

Though the Elmore County gentleman had traveled in Europe and though he might have read Irving's *Sketch Book*, the chances of his having committed the Newcastle inscription to memory were extremely slim. Rather, steeped in the language of the law, which preserves the English of the Magna Charta, Shakespeare, and the King James Bible, and attuned to the rhetoric of the courthouse and the conversation of its corridors, the attorney naturally and unconsciously drew on the great storehouse of our oral speech

---

* Irving, p. 192
** Irving, p. 398, 399
*** Irving, p. 186

traditions, and his paraphrase cleaves to the original in feeling and in style, even to the syllabic and accentual pattern of the substitutions. Though the epitaph as monumental inscription has lost its position as the apex and terminus of our rites for the dead, its echoes still reverberate—in the liturgy and hymnody of Anglo-American Protestantism, in spoken and written eulogies, in memorial verses printed by community and metropolitan newspapers, in oral folk narratives, and in the daily conversation of countless folk personae who, unknowingly—and that is how it should be—with the ease of long, long familiarity, call forth, from an incredibly multifaceted folk memory, the flow, with all its turnings and twistings, of our folk speech.

True, the Duchess of Newcastle and the Elmore County attorney, Ozymandias, Washington Irving, and Shelley, and you, and we, and all who were once named shall, in the day of some remote sun, be unremembered and unnamed, be not even a filament of ash, yet, peradventure, some atom of the language we spoke, some immortal echo of our earthly being, will survive, if only as a sound on the air.

Fig. 11: The girl-child Irma praying on her gravestone.

HISTORICAL PRECEDENTS
FOR ALABAMA EPITAPHS

The epitaph cannot be understood without reference to its historical evolution as a species of inscription which, in its turn, must be studied in the context of the development of language and its expressive rendering, writing. We are accustomed to the constant pouring of words by the billions into hundreds of thousands of libraries, to electronic storage and instant microchip retrieval. Yet, even the most general inquiry into the origins of language, the most cursory glance over the millennia is humbling: from pictogram to hieroglyphics, cuneiform, and the European alphabetic systems; from stones, clay, wood, animal skins, and plant fibers to paper and acrylic screens; from hammer and chisel to pen, press, and photographic negative. For ancient peoples, the inscription was newspaper, religious, civil, and military record and document, the practical medium of thought, knowledge, and experience, and in all these functions, it was everywhere practiced with the skills demanded by any art.

On stone slabs in the markets, on the walls of public and sacred buildings, affixed to statuary, and incised on vases and amphorae, inscriptions set forth treaties, political decrees, prescriptions for rites, commercial transactions, temple offerings, ceremonial duties, honors and accomplishments of citizens, and names, ranks, and battles of military personnel. At Persepolis, Delos, Delphi, Olympia, Ur, Uruk, Troy, Cnossus, Athens, Rome, all along the Nile and the Tigris-Euphrates, archaeologists have uncovered stones bearing thousands of inscriptions. By far most numerous are those on tombs and other memorial structures.

The earliest extant epitaphs, found on Egyptian sarcophagi and coffins, are petitionary prayers to Anubis and Osiris for the dead, together with name, descent, and office. In Classical Greece, where writings on marble show a high degree of letter regularity and vertical and horizontal alignment, most tomb inscriptions contain only the name of the deceased, his father, and *deme,* but some add the age, circumstances of death, and praise or character assessment. Late Republican and early Empire inscriptions of Rome, which set a pattern for all future European capital letters, though similar to their Greek predecessors in simplicity and brevity, exhibit a marked preference for abbreviations and

---

The Sketchbook of Geoffrey Crayon, Gent. New York: The Heritage Press, 1939, "Westminster Abbey," pp. 181-193.

** Sketch Book , p. 393.

Fig. 12: The deeply incised lettering and bold border, ornamented and closed by stylized fleurs de lis, are illustrative of the runic and mystical aspects of carved memorial language.

Fig. 13: A menhir, roughly cut and lettered by a folk hand, evokes the ancient runic power of stones which mark a final resting place for the body and the immortality of the soul.

the beginnings of punctuation, In particular, the Romans used the *dot* to separate words (in use through the latter half of the nineteenth century on English and American tombstones) and the *cross*, (which acquired religious meaning for early Christians) to indicate the beginning of an inscription.

Among the most interesting of all tomb inscriptions are those found throughout Denmark, Sweden, Norway, and England, on great standing stones in the mysterious runic alphabet. Runic is a form of writing which may have originated when Gothic raiders from the Black Sea area came in contact with Greek and Latin writing, becoming thereafter a kind of Germanic folk script used throughout Europe, but especially in Scandinavia, where it was reserved primarily for monumental carving. Located usually in village graveyards, such runic stones were, in the main, abandoned after Christianity became the dominant religion. Though runic writings survive in several alphabets and shapes, and though there is evidence that runic characters were used for legal documents and poetry, their chief purpose was memorial, and the carved symbol itself took on magical and religious properties. In a sense, all tombstone lettering is runic—carved characters inherently empowered to convey the last mystery of man, the sundering of flesh and spirit, and even if we cannot read the alphabet, we may feel its force and assay its meaning.

Further, the very shape of the monument may instantly elicit awareness of its intent. For over three thousand years the same styles have appeared among mankind, archetypal shapes varied only slightly by changing taste, quite as if the folk mind were imprinted with sketches for memorial structures, passing them literally and in the spiritual eye from generation to generation. Among these shapes are: the megalith (large single stone), menhir (tall single standing stone), obelisk (four-sided stone tapering to a pyramidal point), stela (slab), barrow (mound of earth), cairn (mound of stones), sarcophagus and coffin, chambered tomb, house tomb, mausoleum, head stone, foot stone, pillow stone, coping stone, and the cross. Memorial iconography and ornament are similarly apprehended. The evocative force of the figurative expression occurs on the deepest levels of consciousness.

VISUAL ARTS AND THE WRITTEN WORD: A UNIFIED FOLK AESTHETIC

American folk burial arts exhibit a noteworthy historical continuity from the Puritan era to 1950. Those plain folk who rejected all "popish" display developed a fantastical burial style which in its flowering outdid even its most ornate predecessors. Denied worldly pleasures and secular arts, the hungry Puritan consciousness brought forth an entire stone kingdom of the World, the Flesh, and the Devil, of Sin, Time, and Death, of the Soul, Eternity and God, which in thought and execution is overwhelmingly folk. Late Puritan monuments were both architectural—featuring doors, columns, plinths, pedestals and friezes—and sculptural, sometimes even incorporating portraits. Increasingly, they were characterized by elaborate carvings, a New World iconography which would dominate our memorial arts for some time. And though the tradition appears frenzied and various, metaphor, image, symbol, and language are all of one piece. The subtle correspondences between its visual arts and gravestone writings effect a remarkably unified folk aesthetic: a single stone holds the aggregate of Puritan folk literature, sculpture, architecture, philosophy, religion, all realized by artisans of varying competence. Slowly, this exciting gravestone art became less innovative, more stylized, and by 1900 little remained but brilliant remnants.

More than anything else, it is Puritan iconography which is responsible for this wholeness of aesthetic vision and response. The carved symbols and images are derived from Anglo-European folk sources. Scholars point to seventeenth century emblem books, especially Francis Quarles's *Emblemes and Hieroglyphes of the Life of Man* (1639) as the immediate printed repository of the stonecutter's stock in symbols, but their currency throughout Europe and England was universal in folklore, in literature, and in religious art long before the day of Quarles, and they survive to this day. Among them are: images of Time—the burning candle, hourglass, sundial, clock, the scythe; of Death—skeletons, demons, skulls, and crossbones, the death's head and full figure, the summoning angel and the *danse macabre*.

There are symbols drawn from nature, the landscape, and the seasons—trees, vines, flowers, grains, animals, the sun, moon, and stars; personal and organizational symbols—the coat of arms, Masonry, the Knights of Columbus, and various patriotic organizations; figures derived from Christian religion and the Bible—the Book of Life, the scroll of Resurrection, the crown of glory, the sacrificial lamb, the Dove of the Holy Spirit, the Tree of Life, the weeping willow, the blasted tree, the Christian weepers, the New Testament Faith, Hope, and Charity represented by cross, anchor, and heart, the praying hands, the disembodied hand pointing upward to heaven, and even full Biblical scenes; those drawn from hymns, vernacular literature, and folk customs—the open gates, the broken chain

Fig. 14: The Masonic emblem of compass and square appears in relief within a circular medallion.

Fig. 15, above: Funerary art traditionally employed folk motifs, such as a hand with floral tribute emerging from clouds.

Fig. 16, right: Some motifs are derived from Christianity and the Bible—here, a mutilated tree is adorned with flowers and scrolls bearing names of the dead.

Fig. 17: A stylized Tree of Life—weeping willow, recessed from twin scrolls symbolizes both mourning and immortality in this memorial.

link, the sheaf of grain sent by neighbors to a house of mourning, the scallop shell, the serpent, the clasped hands of friendship, the broken column and twin columns, often wreathed and garlanded; and those symbolic devices used primarily as ornamental outline of relief—the rosette, the chain, the swastika, various geometric shapes, grape, ivy, and acanthus vines laden and interwoven with exotic and familiar fruits and flowers, the lily and the rose, pomegranates, pineapple, acorns and other conifers, and, sometimes, animals.

Nearly all these carved symbols have their counterpart in the carved inscription. One example will demonstrate this unanimity of image and inscription and serve to indicate the historical development of American folk death art: that of the angel. The nineteenth century folk epitaph is redolent of these mystical creatures:

In heaven there is one Angel more.

. . .

Gone to be our Angel.

. . .

She faltered by the wayside and the angels took her home.

. . .

It was an angel that visited the green earth
and took the flower away.

Since the early Middle Ages, there have been so many angels that one hesitates to comment on their artistic merit or religious significance—nevertheless, we all know an angel when we see one. The angel of the epitaph is also the angel of the memorial stone, and the direct ancestor of both is the Puritan death's head, which was not always a head, but, like its medieval source, sometimes a torso or complete figure. Whatever the ultimate source of this wondrous image, the death's head is a complex symbol. We are struck with its resemblance to children's drawings, to certain primitive sculpture, and to twentieth century artists like Picasso and Miro, especially in the linear techniques which portray facial expressions. Other than the head, the most prominent feature is wings. And such wings! Nothing on earth like them—the wings of the death angel of long Christian tradition, horrific and benign, the messenger of God, the ethereal creature who invades earth for the body and soul of man and transports it to the grave and immortality.

The Romantic and Victorian successors to the Puritan death angel are serene, pseudo-classical, neuter, childlike or cherubic, blowing trumpets of Doom, bearing wreaths, bouquets, and scrolls, and shorn of terrors, even as the epitaph has shifted from dire warnings and awful afflictions to faith and hope. Smiling vaguely, they bend ever so slightly in an attitude of protection, laying to rest all our nightmares of worms and clay, and if they are less interesting than their predecessors, they are more comforting.

Similar instances of this simultaneity in stone and verbal image may be multiplied. Thousands are the graves of children which read:

Fig. 18a, left: Boy angel praying atop a child's tomb.
Fig. 18b, below: Angelic girl child with bouquet of roses.

Fig. 19, left: A guardian angel reaches a hand to heaven.
Fig. 20, below right: Sword at rest, a saluting angel stands atop a Corinthian column.
Fig. 21, below left: Detail from a wrought iron fence shows the angel of death brooding over mankind, with his scythe ready.

Fig. 22, above left: The tallest object in Marion Cemetery, this guardian angel scatters flowers upon the dead. Fig. 23, above right: Clouds form the background for the ascent of two children and their angel escort to heaven.

A fairer bud of promise never bloomed.

. . .

Budded on earth to bloom in heaven.

. . .

He carries the Lamb in His bosom.

. .

And thousands are the gravestones adorned with the sculpted flower of *Tempus fugit* or with the sleeping stone lamb of innocence, and innumerable are the stone sleeping babes and children in nineteenth century American cemeteries.

FROM ROYALTY TO COMMON FOLK: ALL WANT TO BE REMEMBERED

The poor ghost of Hamlet's father pleads "Remember me," the wish of all mankind, and though the memorial may exist as much, or more, for the sake of the living than for the dead, we have, since the birth of mind, which holds memory, fulfilled that wish. Every tribe and nation which has ever lived on this great globe has set up monuments to those departed this earth, from the monoliths of prehistory, the pyramids of Egypt, and the treasure-laden Norse death ship to the uncut boulders of a small Alabama graveyard. Apart from the mundane convenience of recording a man's life and death, an act which serves history and social organization, the memorial serves art and religion: the epitaphs of this book reflect a religion and an art which are, in substance and style, Anglo-American Christian folk.

The earliest British inscriptions, however, belonged only to royalty—brass tablets were engraved in Latin with the name and rank of the deceased. Not until the time of Elizabeth I were these written in English and the brass engravings displaced by stone monuments. The modern revolution in memorial arts came with the rise of a wealthy mercantile class. One had no need of a title to erect a monument, only money, and by the early eighteenth century there were memorial stone cutters throughout Britain.

In the beginning, these, for the most part, nameless folk carvers were responsible for hewing, lettering, ornamenting, selecting and/or composing inscriptions, but the workshop system developed rapidly in England and America. A company, corporation, or house, often of the same family and continuing for generations, owned or leased quarries and hired apprentices and masters for various specialities. Scholars have now located day books and journals belonging to individual Puritan artisans which contain names of customers, fees, samples of lettering, sketches for design, ornament, and symbol, derived from manuals of iconography and alphabets, but often modified by the carver's skill and personal aesthetic.

Our investigation shows that the cutter of stone memorials remained well within an active vernacular tradition in Alabama until the late nineteenth century. For example, in the Wetumpka City Cemetery several late nineteenth century stones exhibit initials or "marks" and/or the name of the local stone company. Doubtless such artisans were repositories and transmitters of the folk epitaph.

Fig. 24: Innumerable are the sleeping children carved in marble and stone that mark the graves of those who died from childhood diseases of the nineteenth century. The sculpted figure lies within a recessed space which resembles the curtained stage within a proscenium arch.

The Epitaph Defined

Early collectors of gravestone inscriptions created some confusion about the exact nature of an epitaph. Often as not, any memorial writing, especially biographies and eulogies composed for publication and oral delivery, was classified as epitaph, and, thus, many extant specimens derive not from the monuments but print. The *inscription* may be regarded as the total writing on the monument, and the *epitaph* as that part which includes all but name, date, and place of birth and death, and sanguine (blood) and legal relationship ("husband of," "daughter of"). Sometimes a *motto*, either personal or drawn from secular or religious literature, may be carved above the name or below the epitaph. Properly, the motto is not a part of the epitaph, nor is the symbol, whether personal, organizational, religious, or aesthetic, which belongs to the iconography of the monument. The epitaph may be written in prose or verse; it may be of original authorship, known or unknown, or borrowed from other sources, usually those of wide public familiarity. Of varying length, it usually is compatible with the visual qualities of the monument on which it is inscribed. Since most Anglo-American epitaphs belong to a continuous vernacular tradition, questions of origins are difficult. Folklorists have devised motif indexes for songs, tales, riddles, proverbs, games, and superstitions, but, as yet and for obvious reasons, no compendium of folk epitaphs exists. This Alabama collection will show something of their breadth and depth, and although their presentation is helter-skelter and hodgepodge, in the actual manner of their scattered existence, certain recurrent folk genres, themes, motifs, images, and symbols may be identified here.

The Epitaph as Biography

Among the oldest recurring themes is the previously mentioned biographical, a genre derived ultimately from the early Roman inscription. Typically, it included brief biographical information, a petition to the Divine Shades, *D.S.* or *Diis Manibus,* and the statement of burial, *H.S.E., Hic situs est* (Here is situated), later replaced by *Hic jacet* (Here lies). (N.B. The petition *Diis Manibus* is also found in Christian cemeteries, thereby providing a notable example of the strength of folkways, since it is unlikely that the stonecutter was aware that he was perpetuating a pagan tradition.)

Many of the first memorials in America are "Roman" also in their brevity and simplicity, qualities admired by English Neo-Classicists, permitting only the addition of sanguine (blood) and legal relationships. The lengthy biographical and character portrayal of eminent local personages of the late Puritan style became an increasingly important genre throughout the nineteenth century. While the biography is a matter of verifiable historical record, the character summation is idealized, praise is inherent in the description, and the tone is often explicitly didactic. Every community produces a beloved doctor, teacher, or minister, and their epitaphs usually summarize their lives and accomplishments, laud their character, and often, directly or indirectly, urge emulation. The most elaborate of Puritan epitaphs are reserved for the minister who was also often teacher, theologian and statesman. Something of that awe for revered persons is preserved in this tribute to a minister buried in the Wetumpka, Alabama, town cemetery:

> Brother Sawyer was a plain, common sense
> man who turned everything to best account.
> Deeply pious, devoted to his calling, and
> eminently useful wherever he labored.
> He was a man of one business,
> a minister of Christ.

A few miles away, however, in Eclectic, Alabama, is the grave of another local eminent, W. E. Cousins, inscribed simply "The Moses of Elmore." The Old Edwards Cemetery contains an outstanding example of the combined biography and character portrait in the

Fig. 25: Many carvers signed for themselves or their company.

inscription to Elmira Caroline Crenshaw which includes an elegiac poem of original authorship and an extensive comment on her life and personality.

Such epitaphs delight the collector: their language charms, and the character and events enchant, as if we are hearing an old tale of high adventures. The epitaph of Flora McRimmon, buried in the Tuskegee, Alabama, cemetery is a joyous evocation of a great spirited Scottish woman who emigrated to America, survived the Creek Wars, and triumphed over every obstacle save death, to which she succumbed only in her nineties.

Patterns of historical migrations down the Eastern seaboard to Georgia and over into Alabama may be observed in the cemeteries at Auburn, Tuskegee, LaFayette, Montgomery, and Wetumpka, the progress of Jackson's soldiers from South Alabama to Talladega may be mapped in our graveyards. Indeed, all the history of our state and much of that of our nation, our wars, our times of peace and trouble, are all inscribed on our gravestones. To stand beside the grave of Alabama's first governor is to feel history as life, the past as personal and individual, and we cannot but muse over the tender and the tragic, the valorous and the defeated. But the stone never tells the whole tale, and the collector may fill in the gaps with written records in the courthouse and newspaper office, or seek out the legend among local residents who are usually ready enough to relate this murder, that disaster, this affair of love or honor. Failing those resources, the reader of epitaphs may plunder his own imagination, a pleasurable state we often fell into. Hundreds of folk tales and anecdotes cluster about the legendary "Cotton Tom" Heflin, but his epitaph (LaFayette, Chambers County, died 1951) presents an official portrait:

> Attorney, Statesman, Orator, Patriot
> Unawed by opinion
> Unseduced by flattery
> Undismayed by disaster
> He confronted life with antique courage and death with
> Christian hope.

A related genre is the catalog of accomplishments, the most famous example being that of Thomas Jefferson:

> Author of the
> Declaration of Independence
> of the
> Statute of Virginia
> for Religious Freedom
> and Father of the
> University of Virginia

Fig. 26: "Here lies one who in this life was a kind mother and a true wife." Epitaphs such as this one were common in early twentieth century Alabama.

In general, nineteenth century specific portraiture was reserved for eminent personages while ordinary folk had to be content with a brief, conventional character assessment. Among the most widespread are those which honor parents:

A tender mother and a faithful friend.

. . .

She was a kind and affectionate wife, a
fond mother, and a friend to all.

. . .

An affectionate husband, a kind and
indulgent father, brother, and a
friend to all is buried here.

. . .

As a wife, devoted
As a mother, affectionate
As a friend, ever kind and true.

The Woodmen of the World epitaph is a longer, versified variant:

> An amiable father here lies at rest,
> As ever God with his image blest,
> The friend of man, the friend of truth,
> The friend of age, the guide of youth.

One of this type, however, always amuses the contemporary reader, the epitaph for wife and mother: "She hath done what she could." The suggestion is that of the poor, harried lady who hasn't much to do with, but the comedy must be attributed to our ignorance. The allusion is to the beautiful New Testament story of Mary Magdalene, who dries the feet of Christ with her hair and anoints him with expensive perfumes, an act which appears to the disciples immoral. Why does she not use the money for the poor? The rebuke from Christ insists on the necessity of humility and of the symbolic rite: the anointing is prophetic of His death and burial, a memorial to the Magdalene who senses his coming sacrifice, to the dead Christ while he yet lives, and by extension, to all Christian dead.

But the supreme epitaph of the folk as folk, as opposed to epitaphs for the illustrious, is this quatrain:

> This spot contains the ashes of the just
> Who sought no honors and betrayed no trust,
> This truth he proved in every path he trod,
> An honest man's the noblest work of God.

Fig. 27: The tomb of Senator Thomas Heflin is inscribed with an epitaph from Pettigrew's collection of antiquities and inscriptions.

Fig. 28: Plaque affixed to uncut boulder memorializes General Jackson and his Tennessee Volunteers.

(The female version exists also.) The sentiment is peculiarly American, a declared democracy, more, a conscious pride in being an honest man, a word which, since the sixteenth century, has signified not only a moral or ethical quality, but has also served as a designation for the yeomanry. How like the folk, this thumb-your-nose at the great!

THE EPITAPH AS GREETING

Other Roman and medieval gravestone writings appear in this collection. There is, for example, the dialogue of mourner and the dead, *Ave salve* (Hail! Farewell!), and the address to the passerby, *Siste viator* (Pause, wayfarer). For ancient peoples, the funeral was a rite of final farewell. The separations of this century are brief; air transport, the telephone, and satellite communication quickly reunite us, and even our last leavetakings are short. The

Roman soldier, however, left home for months and years, and it was fitting that his salute, at once greeting and farewell, be engraved on monuments. A nineteenth century Christianized variant reads:

> Farewell, my wife and children all,
> From you a father Christ doth call,
> Mourn not for me, it is in vain
> To call me to your sight again.

In medieval England the pagan *Siste Viator* was merged with another species, the *Memento Mori*, the first recorded example said to be that of Edward the Black Prince, in 1321:

> Remember, friend, as you pass by,
> As you are now, so once was I,
> As I am now, so (soon) you will be,
> Prepare for death and follow me.

The iconographical counterparts of *Memento Mori* are the carved death's head, the death angel, and the skull-and-crossbones, all as ubiquitous as the epitaph. So great was its hold on popular taste that several variants evolved. From an Alabama stone dated 1866:

> Remember you that's left behind
> That you must occupy a tomb like mine
> So in life when you fall asleep
> Prepare to meet at Jesus' feet.

The grim secular prophecy has taken on a specifically Christian admonition, and, a bit later, another variant introduces a vein of hope:

> Remember, friends, as you pass by,
> That all mankind were born to die,
> Then let your cares on Christ be cast,
> That you may dwell with him at last.

Many epitaphs specify the manner of death, and in sharp contrast to those "affectionate wives" assessments, here the aim seems to be that of achieving some distinction from the rest of mankind, if only in the circumstances of our leaving. We found several victims of fate, crime, passion, and disease: "Fannie M. Cargile, Killed by a Hit and Run Driver,"

Fig. 29: Twin columns, ornamented with pyramid, united by arch with gable pediment. White Marble.

Fig. 30: Morning glory vine and oak leaf clusters in low relief frame heraldic shield bearing the inscription.

Fig. 31: Pyramid gable carved with wreath of leaves and fruits; note lover's knot and serpentine ribbon.

Fig. 32: Four rosettes, resembling folk crochet and linked by scroll design, ornament this headstone; the incised lettering follows a carved oval, as in a portrait frame.

and on the tombstone of Mary Catherine Carven in Wetumpka, Alabama, the pitiful comment, "Disease, crushing in its power, had long time afflicted her . . ." The death of a soldier in combat is the most common of these circumstantial epitaphs; the gravestone of Captain R. A. Moore reads:

Entered the Confederate service
May 6th, 1862,
was severely wounded in
the Battle of Chickomaugh,
September 20th,
and died in Lowndes County, Alabama,
October 24th, 1863,
in the 34th year of his age.

OCCUPATIONAL EPITAPHS

The "departed" sometimes wish to be remembered for their occupation. English and American epitaphs of the eighteenth and nineteenth centuries often celebrated, sometimes comically, the accomplishments, tools, and skills of various professions and crafts: doctors, lawyers, midwives, clockmakers, blacksmiths, apothecaries, cooks, shoemakers, seamstresses, actors, poets, printers, and newspaper editors. Authored by a village versifier who appropriated the jargon of trades to point a moral, these occupational inscriptions utilize emblematic puns, anagrams, and acrostics which may strike the modern reader as hideously comic or tasteless, but the folk are partial to puzzles and riddles, and we should not be surprised at finding these on their tombs. While several epitaphs in this book are appropriate in diction and style to certain professions, only one (from Wetumpka, Alabama) contains a direct reference to a trade, carpentry, but both language and metaphor derive from the mystic Order of Masonry:

> He met his brethren "upon the plumb"
> and departed with them "in the square."

THE EPITAPH AS BLESSING

Among the oldest, simplest and certainly the most symbolically complex of Anglo-European folk epitaphs is *R. I. P., Requiescat in pace*, "Rest in Peace." Its earliest use occurs on Anglo-Saxon and Danish pillow stones in both Latin, and, significantly, runic characters. Naturally, the folk demanded an English translation of the Latin liturgical phrase, and over the centuries, numerous variants have evolved: "At Rest"; "At Rest in Heaven"; "Weep not, he is at rest"; "At rest with her Father"; "Rest, Soldier Rest/Thy warfare is over"; "Sleep, dearest Willie, and take thy rest." Though all these possess their own strengths, none is so beautiful as "Rest in Peace," for in these three words lie all the terrors and griefs and hopes of man: the language of priest, poet, king, and God, mysterious hieroglyph and mystic rune carved in defiance of the final victor, a wand against despoilers of body and spirit, human utterance raised to its supreme power, an awful, triumphant benediction.

One major innovation clearly observable in early nineteenth century folk gravestone writings is the shift of emphasis from the dead to the bereaved. The sharp edges of fearful admonishment soften, and the epitaph turns consolator. The sentimental tear washes away the stern, the morbid, the comic, the clever, and the original. Versified stanzas on Hope and Loss, Time and Eternity, Memory and Comfort are everywhere, a sort of tombstone greeting card. Sweet cupid cherubs, garlands of flowers, full-bosomed angelic creatures and lovely weepers in flowing robes appear among the uncut boulders, gravehouses, and obelisks, and metaphor, image, symbol, and language progress to a codified set of conventions. Sentimental epitaphs of the nineteenth century violate every aesthetic canon, yet, somehow, they have power to move us, perhaps because of their sheer quantity—the notion of thousands upon thousands of mourners cherishing a verse or saying is in itself endearing. There are those who prize only the costly or the rare or the well-made, and there are those who discover rarity in the commonest of objects, who value whatever is worn

Fig. 33: The crossed swords and inscribed military belt and sash mark the grave of a soldier.

smooth by the touch of hand after hand. For these latter, and for those of the former willing to suspend intellectual judgment, the sentimental epitaph has a thousand charms. Their burden is still remembrance:

> The sweet remembrance of the just
> Shall flourish when they sleep in dust

And by the hundreds of thousands, another folk phrase that has won its own immortality:

> Gone, but not forgotten.

THE EPITAPH AS A METAPHOR FOR HOPE

Wedded to the theme of remembrance are other motifs: the refusal to mourn, the preference for eternity and immortality over time and this world, and the triumph of Christian hope. Recurrent conventional metaphors convey these sentiments, and the scant imagery derives from the common knowledge of the folk, the Bible and Protestant hymnody, natural phenomena, especially time and seasonal cycles, and the stuff of ordinary existence. The theological basis of consolation is acceptance of the will of God, the Dantean "In his will is our peace," which enables the Christian to reconcile the tragic paradox of man's short stay on earth:

> 'Twas hard to give thee up, but thy will be done

and

> God gave, He took, He will restore
> He doeth all things well.

Far less consoling are the words we found on the grave of a child who died in the 1950s:

> If love could have kept her, she would not be sleeping.

A century earlier, however, although loss and sorrow are acknowledged, the dead and the bereaved look towards Heaven:

> A precious one from us is gone,
> A voice we loved is still,
> A place is vacant in our home
> Which never can be filled.
> God in his wisdom has recalled
> The boon His love has given,
> And though the body slumbers here,
> The soul is safe in Heaven.

The vacant place was a favorite Victorian emblem—one thinks of Scrooge's vision of Tiny Tim's empty place by the hearthside. In Tallassee, Alabama, a monument to a young son is a child's chair on which rest his cloak and shoes, the stone equivalent of the vacant-place image of the epitaph. A popular variant associates the coldness of the dead and the voice and name of the deceased with the "sealing" of the soul in the Book of Life:

> The voice we loved is chilled
> His precious name is sealed.

The death of the body as contrasted with the immortality of the soul is prominent in the figure of a casket as holder of treasure, a metaphor which has its counterpart in the

Fig. 34: A founding
father of Montgomery
rests in peace.

Fig. 35: This
biographical
monument tells
the full name,
rank and age of
the deceased,
and that he was
a member of
the 7th U.S.
Cavalry.

tombstone carved to resemble a pall-draped sarcophagus:

> Heaven retaineth now our treasure,
> Earth the lovely casket keeps,
> And the sunbeams love to linger
> Where our sainted mother sleeps.

However, some few brief epitaphs omit all reference to immortality. Amidst all the other consolatory writings, their existential hope stuns:

> His memory is blessed.
> A life to remember.

and the touching:

> Darling, we miss thee.

These are the exceptions; usually, the theme is threefold: that is: loss, remembrance, and Christian comfort:

> Dearest brother, thou hast left us,
> And thy loss we deeply feel,
> But it is God that hath bereft us,
> He can all our sorrows heal.
> To forget thee, dear brother, we can never,
> Love's remembrance lasts forever.

The supremacy of the spirit over flesh is frequently expressed by the warfare metaphor. Numerous stones are engraved with the words of St. Paul in the New Testament: "I have fought the good fight ..." and with the versified folk paraphrase:

> His toils are past, his work is done,
> He fought the fight, his victory won.

This common inscription to husbands and wives utilizes a navigational metaphor for the last journey and that reunion:

> They steered their course to the same quiet shore,
> Not parted long, and now to part no more.

Fig. 36. The belief in a life hereafter is implicit in the words at the bottom of this remarkable iron headstone from c. 1890-1910, "A Crown Without A Conflict."

The final fruit of the Puritan despising of this world is evident here:

> She was too good, too gentle, and fair
> To dwell in this cold world of care.

So much does sleep resemble what we see of dying that it has become a universal symbol of death. For the Christian, sleep and rest represent the passage to eternity. The words "Asleep in Jesus" are inscribed on thousands upon thousands of gravestones, and the entire stanza is in wide occurrence:

> Asleep in Jesus, blessed sleep,
> From which none ever wake to weep;
> A calm and undisturbed repose
> Unawakened by the past of foes.

Another favorite tombstone verse juxtaposes sleep with remembrance of the dead:

> Although he sleeps his memory doeth live.
> And cheering comfort to his mourners give.

Fig. 37: Sarcophagus resting on stone catafalque; the pall is adorned with roses and gathered into pleats by a wide ribband.

Fig. 38: Softly rounded headstone adorned by plaited rim and cross with flowers in relief within recessed medallion; perspective of letters carved beneath follows oval shape of memorial.

Still another contrasts the serenity of sleep-death with the fever and fret of this world:

> No pains, no grief, no anxious fear
> Can reach our loved one sleeping here.

Again, the restful sleep of the dead is set against the turmoil of the bereaved:

> Rest, Mother, rest in quiet sleep
> While friends in sorrow o'er thee weep.

Or, acceptance of death is merged with the metaphor of sleep:

> Sleep on, dear Babe,
> And take thy rest,
> God called thee home,
> He thought it best.

The idea of Heaven as home which abounds in American folk Protestantism is also prevalent in the nineteenth century epitaph. The Christian is a pilgrim journeying through a vale of tears, the "poor, way-faring stranger," journeying upwards towards eternal bliss. In the great American folk hymn of that name, the exile proclaims:

> There'll be no sickness, toil or danger
> In that bright land to which I go

as does this epitaph:

> Gone to a bright home
> Where grief cannot come.

On the grave of a Scottish immigrant in Tuskegee, Alabama, are these piteous words:

> Blessed are they that are homesick,
> For they shall come to their father's house.

But, the finest of all the home epitaphs, and perhaps of all American folk memorial literature, is simply:

> Gone Home

Fig. 39: Thousands of gravestones bear similar inscriptions.

Fig. 40: Bedstead tomb of brick masonry.

All of us at some time have felt the longing for home. Inexplicably, when we ourselves are mothers and fathers or grandparents, of a sudden, we are filled with an unbearable desire to go home—a certain streak in the sky, the scent of some spice, a tree at a crossroads, a weave of cloth, a phrase, even a single word, and the need overpowers all reason. The very old and dying say "I wish I could eat at my mother's table one more time," and the troubled child cries "I want to go home." Small wonder that churches celebrate annual rites of Homecoming, a reunion of the folk community when those who have been scattered abroad come back for fellowship, or that the word homecoming holds for us such tender associations. The returning soldier, the college student, the young married couple, all dream of going home, and, at the dawn of the third millennium, multitudes are literally and spiritually homeless. This brief memorial inscription, drawn from living American folk speech, reverberates with the passionate yearning of a whole nation of wanderers— Gone Home.

Another "home" epitaph loved by the American folk suggests the New Testament metaphor of Christ as the Good Shepherd:

> Jesus has come and borne her home.

Closely tied to the Good Shepherd motif is the image of arms. The metaphor of God as "the everlasting arms," the signification of Divine protection and strength prominent in the Old Testament, was transformed by medieval Christian literature into the morbid embrace of those unlikely lovers, the soul and the grave or Death. That motif survives in this stanza from a fine old American hymn which is sometimes carved on gravestones:

> I will arise and go to Jesus,
> He will embrace me in his arms.
> In the arms of my dear Saviour,
> O, there are ten thousand charms.

The erotic death image is muted in this epitaph:

> Dearest one, I have laid thee
> In the peaceful grave's embrace;
> But thy memory I will ever cherish
> Till I see thy heavenly face.

"Safe in the arms of Jesus" appears in every cemetery we ever visited. A touching variant from the town cemetery at Dadeville, Alabama, reads:

> Our sweet little girl is safe in the arms of Jesus,
> Waiting and watching for Papa and Mama.

Folk art and literature which memorialize the child bear special significance in the nineteenth century. Romantic and Victorian writers were preoccupied with the child as poet, visionary, and as emblem of both mystic knowledge and incorruptible innocence, and such concepts surely existed, if unconsciously, in the American folk. Since the first settlements at Jamestown, children had been victims of disease, starvation, harsh environment, and by 1850, of an even harsher industrial exploitation. Thousands upon thousands were stillborn, died in infancy or in early childhood—their names and graves are legion. Their idealization in folk epitaphs is everywhere, and the sorrow of their deaths is a distinctive pain. Here, in both the literary and stone memorials, is a sorrow like no other, and a love past all forgetting—a cradle of rocks, a coverlet of mussel and oyster shells, or colored marbles, and the tender sayings carved on stone beds:

> Our babe
> . . . . .
>
> Suffer the little children
> . . . .

She was the sunshine of our home

. . . . .

For the rest, the nineteenth century epitaph is chiefly scriptural and religious; passages are extracted from practically every book in the Bible, although Job, the Psalms, Proverbs, the Beatitudes, and the writings of Paul are preferred. Following close are phrases from the Anglican (and other Protestant) service for the dead and lines from Christian hymns— "Pass me not, O, Gentle Savior"; "When the roll is called up yonder, I'll be there"; "Earth has no sorrow that Heaven cannot heal." Church membership is often carved on memorial stones, as in these words on the grave of Elvey Locke in Orion:

She joined the Baptist church in 1819,
where she remained in full faith and fellowship
until her much lamented death.

Such nineteenth century religious epitaphs are much more than lip service to a prevailing moral and social order. Taken in their entirety and read over and over, time and again, in all weathers and seasons, from town to town, from cemetery to cemetery, they possess a tragic sense, beyond description, of man's fate, his brotherhood with other men, the courage and joy of his brief stay on earth, his mortal loss and pain, and his sure and certain hope of immortality:

Blessed are the dead who die in the Lord.

. . . . .

Mark the perfect man and behold the upright,
for the end of that man is peace.

. . . . .

Let me die the death of the righteous and
let my last end be like his.

. . . . .

Then shall the dust return to the earth and
the spirit unto God who gave it.

Now and again the nineteenth century epitaph derives from some well or little known author: Tennyson's "Crossing the Bar" is far and away the favorite, and Mark Twain's choice for his daughter, a poem not by Twain, as is commonly supposed, but by Robert Richardson of Australia, is a modern version of Martial's *Sit tibi terra levis* (Light be the earth upon thee):

Fig. 41: Child's grave with coverlet of mussel shells.

Warm summer sun, shine kindly here
Warm southern wind, blow soft by here.
Green sod above, lie light, lie light,
Good night, dear Daddy, good night.
Goodnight.

More frequent is the tribute, usually versified, composed by one of the bereaved or by the dead:

Your life with us was warm and good
but brief . . .
Like a gentle wave upon the sandy beach.
We love you still, your light shines on,
Brightly,
But just beyond our reach.
For Martha Jane Smith
8 years old
Written by her uncle,
James O'Neal

* * *

Farewell, friend, yet not farewell,
Where I am gone, ye too shall dwell.
I am gone before your face
A moment's time, a little space;
When you come where I have stepped,
Ye will know by wise love taught
That here is all and there is naught.
Written by Pearl.

While the many various translations and versions of the Bible since 1930 may serve the ends of accuracy and comprehension, the decline of the King James Version in pulpit and readership has resulted in the steady weakening of a great common bond among the folk. For over three hundred years this Bible was our Book of Books, our only book, a folk literary treasury, storehouse and source of our folk poetry and song, folk saga and history, our fables, riddles, proverbs, our folk heroes, saints, warriors, and kings, not to speak of its role in the shaping of a common folk religious tradition or the formulation of theological dogma. Moreover, its language unified and kept cohesive these traditions, so that whether or not the folk understood its intellectual substance, we readily perceived the rest, its overtones and nuances, and its rhythms, syntax, and vocabulary permeated our daily discourse. Hence, we must read these epitaphs from the King James Bible not as mottos or as we read any other literary quotation, but as the living, revealed word of God cut on the stones of remembrance.

THE EPITAPH AS A WINDOW TO THE PAST

Here, in this Platonic Alabama graveyard rest those we have come to cherish as old friends: Charity Newsom, "Safe in the arms of Jesus"; Sallie E. Grace, "The Soldier's Friend"; maid Helen who "touched our hearts and quainted us with Heaven"; Hiram E. Stoddard, "Honorable and upright in every relation of life"; Elias Jenerett, "Sweetly sleeping"; Mary A. Howell, "brave with the high spirit of the Old South"; Col. Howell Rose, "the architect of his own fortune"; Pleasant Buckner whose "many virtues form the noble monument to his memory"; and little Mattie Mera, "Gone so soon!"

Here are good wives, loving mothers, and charming ladies: the remarkable Leir Journigan, 86 years, "the wife of three husbands, the mother of 18 children, and died with but few silver hairs crowning her head"; Elizabeth Clarke De Fee whose "ways were ways of pleasantness and all her paths were peace"; Queen Ester Jordan whose epitaph is the prayer of the thief crucified with Christ, "Lord, remember me when Thou comest into Thy Kingdom"; Martha E. Walden, "Her children rise up and call her blessed"; Sara Louise Crenshaw, "Few women ever gave more that was good and asked or expected less of this world"; and Aunt Jane Worthington, "Aged 85 years, she lived for others . . ."

Fig. 42: The mourner, sculpted within a garlanded alcove, clasps an elongated cross and bears a box of spices; she is symbolically identified with the three women present at the Crucifixion and Resurrection, especially Mary Magdalene who ritually anointed the feet of Christ during his last days on earth and who was the first to encounter him as the Risen Lord.

We have heard the last sad lullaby and prayer for a dead child:

> Go to thy rest, fair child,
> Go to thy dreamless bed,
> While yet so young and undefiled,
> With blessings on thy head.

and the sound of grief as natural, heartbroken conversation in this tribute to Mike who died in 1919:

> His gentle, young life was one of extreme
> Kindness and affection to Mama, Papa, and Friends.
> He did his best to make us happy and proud of him.

We have sorrowed for John Richard Wiggins:

> The youth hath died in a strange land

and followed Thomas and Rebecca Williams in three long processions to offer up the bodies of their infants:

> We lay our children in the tomb,
> In faith their spirits at thy feet we see

and looked hard at the stone covering little Mollie Russell who lived only twelve days:

> A little time on earth she spent.

*Fig. 43, left:
The simplest of Christian epitaphs.*

Fig. 44, below: Bible verses were often inscribed in their entirety, and in the language of the King James Version.

Fig. 45: The souls of the faithful enter the New Jerusalem; the Crown looming large over the Heavenly City represents both Christian triumph of life over death and God, creator and ruler over this world and the next.

On the massive marble dedicated to the maiden Lena Schuessler, we read of a short life marred by constant pain and watched her peaceful end:

> Fair spirit, rest thee now.

Again and again, we hear Mariah Ann Shepherd calling to her children:

> Rise, children, rise from the encumbrance of clay;
> Give heed to my call, Come away, Come away.

Often we breathed the air of a young state and land, as at the grave of Colonel Charles McLemore, a member of the General Assembly of Alabama:

> He was gifted and brilliant, gentle but knightly,
> and no truer patriot sleeps beneath the sod of Alabama.

We knew surely that Jessie McKinley Stokes could not have been born anywhere except

Between Ridgefield and Devil's Half Acre, Coosa County near Rockford.

We tipped a hat to

John Ellis McNeill, 46th Ala, Fought in 27 Battles,
Unscratched, Died in 1867.

Elkanah Barnes, stern and proud, cried out the epitaph he himself wrote:

I am an honest man, Elkanah Barnes.

The sturdy Scot Malcolm McInnis appeared before our very eyes:

He stood four square to every wind that blew.

We craved for our own this tribute to the uprightness of Shadrack Thompson:

With life and name unstained, a good man dies.

We yearned to speak with Araminta E. Collins, 1858-1911:

The law of truth was in her mouth. And she walked with God in peace.

Coincidentally, just at sundown in the Auburn City Cemetery, we read on the gravestone of William Leroy Brown:

The sun of a well spent day is spent
Quiet has come forever
And forever peace.

The inscriptions on the tombs of Ira J. and Pricilla Tucker, husband and wife, hymns of their faith, fitly express the entire folk Christian tradition of the epitaph:

O sing to me of Heaven
When I am come to die
Sing songs of holy ecstasy
To waft my soul on high.

Fig. 46, above left: Mourner in 19th century Gothic Revival tomb.

Fig. 47, below left: Table monuments: stela supported by classical columns.

Fig. 48, above right: Cathedral architecture monument: rounded arches rising to semi-Gothic point with urn finial; spool columns enclose a second urn; base carved as menhirs for inscriptions.

Fig. 49, below right: Ornate Gothic spire topped with Cross (a detail of the Gothic tomb in Fig. 46 above).

Fig. 50: Marble monument with relief carving of angel wings and wreath, an uncommon symbol.

But no gravestone writing has ever moved us as this one from an unlettered hand and noble heart:

Preshers Memerey

Glorey to God

What, after all, is in a word? And what's in a name? A very great deal. In Arthur Miller's *The Crucible*, when John Proctor is urged to sign a false confession of witchcraft, he shouts, "But it is my name!" The commonness of the folk epitaph is beautifully countered by the uniqueness of the name, that powerful alphabetic configuration which cries out a distinct human identity. More than anything else throughout this long investigation, we have been impressed with the strange power of a name carved on stone. Beyond the first musings over a man's life and days, comes an uncanny feeling of having known the dead, their comings and goings on this earth, and often, for some unknown reason, the association between the name and the epitaph will evoke a human presence. This awareness has nothing to do with the travesty of talking to the dead, in or out of graveyards. The tedious process of recording, editing, and arranging, of returning again and again to a single inscription, partly explains our feelings. We have lived a long time with these writings, we know these dead, and it is only natural that we grow fond of certain names and sayings. But that is not all of it: on any cemetery visit, a certain stone will beckon one of us, and we will gather there to read and wonder. Some peculiarity in carving, decoration, lettering, the shape of a stone, a tree nearby, a fence, something, draws us there, and though we may forget the cemetery or community, we will remember the spot and the name. These names have gone home with us—and these names have gone home.

Fig. 51: Inscriptions may contain several different typefaces forming words that may be curved in placement.

A Note on the Lettering

Frederick Burgess made a notable beginning in the investigation of gravestone lettering in his 1963 volume *English Churchyard Memorials*. He sketches the outlines of its historical development as follows:

• the Roman-British epoch characterized by classical spacing and proportion, with linked and encircling letters used as decoration;

• the Anglo-Saxon and Norman period which, though scant evidence survives, exhibits in Welsh crosses the use of Irish half-uncials and, after 1066, the mixed square and rounded letters from the continent;

• the 13th century Lombardic style, adapted from manuscript illumination and appearing as both incised and recessed for lead or brass filler;

• the very late 14th century Gothic, marked by the appearance of both upper and lower case letters and by the Carolingian half-relief script, notable for cross-barred A's, looped C's and D's, the double V for W, and bars ornamented with knots, spurs, or forked extremities;

• the 17th century Neo-Classic style;

• 18th century diversity, distinctive for the wedge-shaped chisel forms resembling stencil and calligraphic lettering derived, in the main, from the Roundhand and Chancery handscripts and practiced by engravers who studied George Bickham's *The Universal Penman* (1743);

• the continued multiplicity of styles in the 19th century, including display types, three dimensional or shadowed lettering, Gothic revival elements and Victorian calligraphy;

• and, finally, the chisel-cut Trajan Column alphabet of modern times.

This development of lettering, calligraphy, handscript, and type from ancient Rome to the present is unquestionably reflected in the Alabama gravestones we have seen and studied for nearly three decades.

Though our aim was simply to gather epitaphs, we came in time to discover the wholeness of memorials, their inseparableness, a mingling of various elements which, whether by accident, design, or even the ravages of time, renders to a gravestone its own being. Every stone, though similar to hundreds of others, has a different name and a different *feeling* about it, something which emanates, perhaps, from those whom it honors and from their bereaved, from its maker, from its time, its place, and its aspect or situation, hillside, valley, town, churchyard, or city. In time, memorials become part of the landscape, and that these should take on the look of the earth, that they should sink, twist, fade, lean, accommodating themselves in thousands of small ways to wind and rain and sun, is, somehow, right, for nothing so afflicts the spirit as the nakedness of new stones, like the rawness of new grief. Nowhere does written language seem more a part of nature than on a gravestone. There it loses its remoteness, and by and by, warms to the palpable, the tangible, acquires a living shape—Shakespeare's sea-change, "Of his bones are coral made/ Those are pearls that were his eyes."

Our discovery of wholeness, the individuality of each stone, and of the transmutation of language to a new, higher power led, somehow, to the decision to hand-letter these Alabama inscriptions. When the typist gave us her first pages, we were shocked at how diminished were the epitaphs, how shorn of spirit, mutilated, faceless, shadowy, pitifully bare of the blessedness we felt in their natural setting. These writings represent an historical millennium of dreams, fears, sorrows, defeats, joys, and triumphs of the folk. More importantly, whatever is immortal in man speaks to us from these stones and its evocation in a book called for a hand.

It occurred to us that a calligrapher might best present these inscriptions, but, one day as we pondered over the original manuscripts and encountered scores of different

Fig. 52: Raised lettering and vine leaf carved as encircling wreath.

Fig. 53, above: Tombstone displaying multiple decorative motifs and incised lettering.

Fig. 54, right: Raised lettering.

handwritings came the idea of a folk handscript. Over the years, the penmanship of numerous old manuscripts has fascinated us—letters, diaries, account books, minutes of meetings, legal documents. As school children, we were given only rudimentary instructions in penmanship, but our parents and grandparents practiced it all their lives. To say "He writes a good hand" or a pretty, or beautiful, or fair hand was once to bestow a compliment, to pay homage to the advantages of a liberal education, to recognize a skill possessed by the relatively few, for, as late as 1930 in America, thousands could not read or write, and clerks and copyists were in great demand. To this day, in my hometown, people still talk of the beautiful penmanship of Miss Dora Wendel. Such practitioners perpetuated certain textbook styles which may be widely observed in nineteenth century manuscripts. Not surprisingly, each penman exhibits his own peculiarities, and, thus, the

Fig. 55, above: Incised lettering.
Fig. 56, right: Incised lettering in different typefaces.

varieties of handscript are almost limitless.

The notion that epitaphs might be presented in folk handwriting grew into a conviction. Since I was the one at home, at odd moments I assayed it, though we would have preferred to have many hands in the work. We wanted a script which recalled both nineteenth century penmanship and gravestone lettering, so that reading this book would be a little like viewing the actual stones. I was guided by some general observations of lettering on Alabama gravestones:

• Most letters are recessed and the deeper the cut, the longer they are readable, but a few are carved in low relief;

• The most prominent style is bold Roman in varying sizes, slants, and thicknesses;

• The Gothic, in all its forms, is rare, but less rare than one might suppose;

• The back hand in a mixture of several folk styles is widely current;

• The Chancery cursive and the slanted Italic, both in capitals and lower case, is well represented;

• Uniformity in height and spacing is impressive, though vowels are often lower or higher than consonants;

• A line may follow the shape of the stone or may be arranged in some arbitrary manner, the most common being a partial circle;

• Most lines give the appearance of perfect horizontals and verticals but slant imperceptibly;

• Serifs and decorative extremities, of every kind, are very common and the use of all capitals is rare;

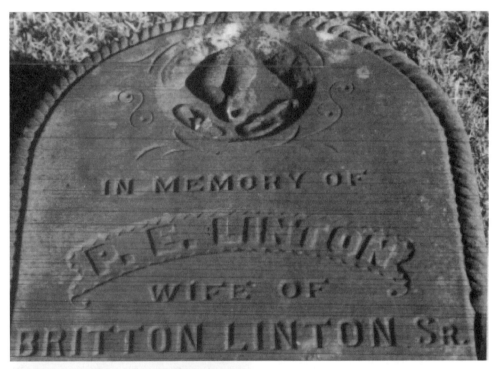

Fig. 57, above: A combination of raised and incised lettering, used with the broken chain motif, a carved rope border, and various incised designs. Fig. 58, left: Simple incised lettering.

• Any given style will reflect an overall principle of, say, roundness, squareness, crowding, or spaciousness, and flourishes and other decorative aspects will possess a distinctly individual quality;

• Indentations and other spatial arrangements follow traditional folk patterns of centering, both to the horizontal and the vertical, and these may or may not be mathematically regular, but, in most cases, give the appearance of regularity;

• Abbreviations of names, places, and of years, months, and days are common;

• Both improper and proper hyphenation may be found, but not in abundance;

• The lettering of the epitaph may be consistent with size, spacing, and arrangement of all the other lettering, but, in general is smaller and of a different style;

• From two to five or six different penmanship styles may be observed on one stone;

• End punctuation is generally present, but is often absent on stones c. 1750 to 1880;

• The order of presentation is nearly always (1) the call to memory (*Here lies* or *Sacred to the Memory of*) of the name of the dead, (2) sanguine and legal relationships, (3) the birth and death dates, (4) the motto, and (5) the epitaph, though these two last may be reversed;

• The initials or name of the carver or the company may sometimes be discovered in

Fig. 59: The (wrought iron) gates opening to the dome of heaven beneath the Anchor of Hope and the benediction of peace.

the lower left or right hand corner, and emblems appear at various places on the stone;

• Correctness in spelling and grammar is overwhelmingly evident, but folk deficiencies in these areas may be easily documented;

• The lettering, often highly skilled and of no little artistic merit, evidences the predilection of the individual carver.

Some of these principles are incorporated in the handscript of this volume, but I had no method. Over those years more love and labor went into numerous experiments with pens and papers than skill and ability. The scribbling went on and on and thousands of scribbles went into the wastebasket. Sometimes a name called forth a certain lettering, sometimes the mood of the epitaph, again the biographical circumstances, but always there was some difference from all the other inscriptions, and that distinction determined the manner of writing. In retrospect, I think I wished only to offer an intimation of the stone and the human life which it memorialized. Now and then there were moments of pure pleasure, but there were hours of miserable frustration, and every failure seemed an affront, even a humiliation to my fellows. By a strange twist, the collector of folklore and life was transformed into a folk artisan, or, at any rate, I had such pretensions, and I began to know a little of what it is like to piece a quilt, to have a go at some great undertaking in embroidery, the careful stitch by stitch, the few gestures of ease and freedom, the dispassionate facing up to errors and flaws, the ripping out and starting all over again. I thought of Chaucer's "The life so short, the craft so hard to learn," and despair rode me, and still does, but out of it all came my first understanding of the folk artist—how reach exceeds grasp, how limitations in skill, gift, time, and energy always stifle, shadow, and cripple, how the vision in mind and heart is never fully realized. Yet, here and there, some piece seemed good, and I kept at it. As matters have turned out, only some of those scribbles were selected for this book, but no matter, for nothing is ever truly wasted. Quilt, dulcimer, painting, tin can and bottle tree, or whatever, we all need to make something outside the self that will yet be the self. Though it may miss the mark, a little or ever so wide, though it may be received with scorn and derision, contempt or pity, by those who are more gifted or wise, a folk art is extraordinary by reason of its maker, the ordinary person who yearns after some vision of beauty. That the dream does not come true, may be, after all, beside the point. Like the Magda who anointed the feet of Christ, all the folk do what we can. It may not be much, but it'll do. Will do for the yearning, or at least signify what we would do, had we the means, for if we had our way, our making would be more precious than jewels, and eye could not see, nor ear report, nor tongue tell its marvels.

— Olivia Solomon

THE EPITAPHS

Here Lies Our Darling Gena
The Idol of our Hearts

Sacred to the Memory of

Eugenia C. Cook

who was born Aug. 7, 1845
and departed this life
Aug. 24, 1865
Aged 20 yrs. and 17 ds.

Darling, by thy grave oft times we'll stand;
And weep to know that thou art gone.
But yet we'll hope, in that bright heavenly land
To meet our Gena, when life is done.
She is gone, and forever her life's sun is set,
But its golden beams linger to comfort us yet;
She has gone in the fullness of beauty and youth,
An emblem of virtue, a witness of truth.
Like a bright blooming flower
Whose root was on high,
She has faded from earth
But still blooms in the sky.

Old Union Cemetery

To The Memory of
The Pioneer Settlers of
Ebenezer Community
and the Soldiers of
Company E 33 D
Alabama CSA

In Memorium, By Her Mother,
of Jessie, only child of
   Joulbert and Parthenia
      Hatcher
and wife of Julius P. Oliver
Born Oct. 4, 1843 and died Jan. 10, 1870
This humble tribute of her parent's love
Not only marks the spot where now she lies
But warning gives to all who strove to seek
In Death their home beyond the skies.

Joulbert Hatcher
Born in Greene Co. Ga. Sep 7, 1806
Died in Dadeville, Ala. Jan 25, 1877
All, all are gone, the good, the fair,
All lost in life's sweet bloom,
And I in rage might claim thy care,
Survive to raise thy tomb.

      Parthenia   Wife of Joulbert Hatcher
      Born May 3, 1816 and died July 26, 1905
         Our Grandmother Hatcher
         Dadeville Cemetery

Infants of W.A. and M.E. Porch
Born and Died
April 25, 1879

Infant Daughter of
W.A. and M.E. Porch
Born and Died
November 2, 1880

Three little shepherds lie side by side
Beneath the churchyard sacred sod
But those who sleep in the desert or deep
Are watched by the self-same God.

One little sister and two little brothers
Are laid beneath these earthly clods:
Oh, do not weep, my mother,
You know your little ones are with God.

Red Ridge
Methodist Church
Cemetery

Tallapoosa
County
Alabama

Fannie Lou
Dau. of
B. W. and E. A. Starke
Born Oct. 7, 1871
Died Apr. 29, 1891

Fairest flower of earthly blooms,
A blossom filled with rich perfumes,
No sweeter fragrance e'er was given
Neath the shining courts of Heaven.

Immortal bloom: in glory's shrine,
Enraptured soul: in realms divine,
Loved on earth and loved in Heaven,
Oh, how sweet the assurance given.

Unselfish may your parents prove
Sustained by Heaven's unbounded love
Trusting in God our home shall be
At last, our darling, in Heaven with thee!

Reunited in glory! How blissful the thought!
Known only by those whom our
                    Saviour hath bought.
Even so mote it be.
                    Even so mote it Be.
                         Oakwood Cemetery

In Memory of
Harris Nicholson
A Revolutionary
Soldier
who was born on the
12th day of March
in the year A.D. 1760
and departed this life
the 28th day of June
in the year A.D. 1841
Aged 81 yrs 11 mos 6 ds

John W. Nicholson
who was born on the 2nd
day of October in the year
A.D. 1829 and departed
this life on the 10th day
of September 1851.
Aged 21 yrs 11 mos 8 ds
He was a consistent
member of the M.E. Church
and died in the Christian
faith.

Mary M.
Consort of
James Nicholson
who was born on
the 27th day of Mar.
in the year A.D. 1793
and departed this
life on the 10th
day of July in the
year A.D. 1841.
Aged 48 yrs 3 mos
13 ds

She attached herself
to the M.E. Church
in early life and
died as she had lived
in the Christian
faith. Blessed are
they that die in
the Lord.

Tuskegee
Cemetery

Sacred to the Memory of

Mrs. Catherine

Consort of

Capt. William Ott

who departed this life

Jan 9 1847

in the 61st year of her life

Could love unbounded have witheld thy soul,
From Heaven we now would feel thy mild control,
For ne'er till time's last light
Shall cease to be,
Will live a being
More Beloved than Thee.

Oh, ne'er till world on world shall all expire,
And Earth be one vast sea of liquid fire,
Shall pass a spirit to its native sky
More fit to live,
More prepared to die.

Miller's Tabernacle
Cemetery

Sacred to the Memory of
Elvey Locke
4th wife of Rich. Locke and
dau. of John Dearer, past of
Burke Co. Georgia
who was born Nov. 3, 1792
and died Mar. 28th, 1836

She was married to Rich. Locke
the 3rd of March, 1812. She
joined the Baptist Church in 1819,
where she remained in full faith
and fellowship until her much
lamented death.
    Therefore, the Redeemed of the Lord
shall return and come with singing unto
Zion; and everlasting joy shall be upon
their heads. They shall obtain gladness
and joy; And sorrow and mourning
        shall flee away.
    Orion Baptist Church Cemetery

George P.
Son of
J.M.R. and A.D. Reid
who was born in Crawfordville
Talliaferro Co. Ga.
May 6 1847
and died
May 26 1857

Fate gave the word, the arrow sped
And pierced my darling's heart,
And with him all joys are fled
Life can to me impart.
Yet again we hope to meet thee
When the day of life is fled,
Then in Heaven with joy to greet thee
Where no farewell tear is shed.
Old Edwards Cemetery

Mike
Son of
W. P. and L. C. Huey
Aug 4 1900
Sep 25 1919
His gentle young life
was one of extreme
Kindness and Affection
to Mama, Papa, and Friends.
He did his best to make
us happy and proud of him.
Carter Cemetery

Queen Esther Jordan
Feb. 14, 1884
Jan. 23, 1958
Lord, remember me
when Thou comest
into Thy Kingdom.
Ramah Cemetery

L. B. Armstrong
Born
12th August 1827
Died
13th December 1851
Ille, quum praestantie
suae magnam spem
feeiset, prime ex
X tinctus in acuo.
Talladega Cemetery

Maude Helen
Inf. Dau. of
H. H. and Maude Smith
Born Sep. 28, 1904
Died in Auburn, Ala.
Dec. 1, 1905
She touched
our hearts
and quainted us
with Heaven.
Pine Hill Cemetery

In Memory of
Flora
the widow of William Fraser

She was born in 1755 on the Isle of Skye, Scotland, of the sect McRimmon, hereditary pipers to the Cloin McLeod.

Was one of the colony of Culloden Scotch in North Carolina and a resident of Kershaw District, South Carolina where she lost her husband: There with her children she joined the pioneers of Eastern Alabama and built with her own hands the first church in that region: She survived the Creek outbreak of 1836 being warned by the Uchle Indians and lived at Wattula, Ala. until 1846 when she died at the age of 91 years.

In this grave be also the remains of her grandson William Fraser, native of Louisiana and a soldier of the Confederacy who died at Watulla, Ala. in 1864 aged 24 years of sickness contracted in that army.

Tuskegee Cemetery

Sacred to the memory of
Capt. R. A. Moore
who was born July 9th, 1831
Entered the Confederate service
May 6th 1862. Was severely wounded
in the Battle of Chickomaugh Sep. 20
and died in Lowndes Co., Ala. Oct. 24th
1864 in the 34th year of his age.

As an officer, he was greatly beloved
by his men; as a Husband, he was the
idol of his wife; as a Christian, he was
a shining light; and as a man, he
had not an enemy.

This monument was erected
by his friends as their
testimony to his
excellent and illustrious
character.

Little Sandyridge Cemetery
Sandyridge, Alabama

Jessie McKinley
Stokes
Born 1893
Between Ridgefield
and
Devil's Half-Acre
Coosa County
near Rockford
Bullard Cemetery

Not all the dead forgotten lie:

In Memory of Reverend Elvon O. Martin

A faithful and beloved minister of

the Gospel who was born in

Underhill, Vermont

April 18th, 1806

and died in peace at

Sandyridge, Lowndes Co., Alabama

March 3rd, 1845

This marble is furnished by his affectionate people and friends who esteemed
and lov'd him while living and honor
his memory now dead.

    Dear pastor, husband, father, friend, head,
we loved thee living and we mourn thee dead
Why should we weep? For all his gracious word,
Thou'rt absent from the flesh –

    But present with the Lord.

Also, Margaret Lucinda, his infant
daughter who lies by his side,
aged 15 months.

Little Sandyridge
Cemetery

Sacred to the memory of
William Wyatt
Bibb
Died 10th of July 1820
in the 40th yr. of his age

He was the first governor of the
territory and afterwards of the State
of Alabama. He was the eldest son of
William and Sally S. Bibb and was born
in Prince Edward County, Virginia.

Dear departed shade, thy many
virtues will long be treasured in the
memory of thy numerous friends.
And though they mourn thy early fall,
they are consoled with the hope that
thou art at rest in the bosom of the
Heavenly Father. Such, alas, is the
uncertain stage of human —

(the rest is unreadable)

Bibb Cemetery
Elmore County, Alabama

In Memory of
Ira J. Jucker
Born Dec. 4, 1815
Died Jan. 21, 1880
Aged
64 yrs 1 mo 17 ds

Jesus can make a dying bed
Feel soft as downey pillows are
While on his breast I lean my head
And breathe my life out sweetly there.

In Memory of Priscilla
Wife of Ira J. Jucker
Born Jan. 6, 1821
Died July 20, 1862

O, sing to me of Heaven
When I am come to die
Sing songs of holy ecstasy
To waft my soul on high.

Fairview Cemetery
Eufaula, Ala.

Sacred to the Memory of

Mary Veasey
Wife of Elijah Veasey

who was born
Feb. 7, 1818
and who died
Feb. 6, 1810

Hear what the voice from Heaven doth acclaim
For all the pious dead:
Sweet is the savour of their name
And soft their sleeping bed.
They die in Jesus and are blest,
How kind their slumbers are!
From suffering and from sin released,
They are freed from every snare.

Red Ridge Methodist
Church Cemetery
Tallapoosa, Co., Ala.

Hugh K. Hall
Co. A
47th Ala. Inf.
C. S. A
Born 1808
Died Oct. 1895

His life has been a sermon
And his name will be a text
To point from this world's honor
To the glory of the next.

From the land he loved so well
He goes where only it is given
To know of fairer scenes and climes,
The atmosphere of
Heaven.

Red Ridge Methodist Church Cemetery
Tallapoosa County
Alabama

Sacred to the Memory of
Sarah Louise Crenshaw
Wife of Frederick W. Crenshaw
Born January 26, 1842
Died September 5, 1911
They that trust in the Lord shall be as
Mount Zion which cannot be removed but
abideth forever.

She had a spirit which elevated mere manners into
love and Kindness, and she had that rarest gift of a
Christian, the power to make piety an enchantment
for those about her. She was a mother who never weaned
her children, but nurtured them to the last with courage
and peace. She made a home that was a Heaven, and she
had a genius for hospitality so grave in its simplicity
so warm in its silence, that one felt her expectations
of the 'angel unawares.'

Few women ever gave more that was
good and asked or expected less of the world.

Crenshaw Family Cemetery
Butler County, Alabama

Sacred be this monument
to the memory of

Reverend Robert Holman
Late Pastor of the First Presbyterian
Church of this city

Passenger, of whatever name, attend,
for here rest the remains of one who as a
soldier was active, brave; and vigilant as
a citizen; was social, free, and liberal as
a Christian. The minister was bold and
ardent and of deep-toned piety ascerting
on all proper occasions the majesty and
lovingkindness of his God and exhibiting
in all his conduct the simplicity of the
Gospels. Let us rejoice at the memory; and
Example yet lives which is worthy of
all Imitation.
Born in Kent in 1801, died in New
Georgia, 1841.
Erected by the young men of the city of Wetumpka

Wetumpka Cemetery
Wetumpka, Alabama

Sacred to the Memory of
James Herren
Son of Alexander Herren
Born in Jasper Co. Ga.
Apr. 25, 1798
Departed this life
Nov. 8, 1856

For 32 years in sickness and in health he was a faithful member of the M.E. Church, South, and died in holy triumph of a — faith.

His Wife Tabitha

She lived and died
trusting her lord
and her last words were
Oh, Jesus, take me to
Thyself. I'm going now
to Heaven.

His Wife Ann

We loved her
in life,
Let us not
forget her
in death.

Camp Hill
Cemetery

Leir Journigan
1780 - 1866
She was the wife of three
husbands and the mother of
eighteen children and died with
but few silver hairs
crowning her head.
Having finished life's duty, she
now sweetly rests.

Chapel Hill Baptist Church Cemetery

In Memory of
Mary Sabina Samuel
Daughter of
Chaˢ P. and Eliza B. Samuel
Born July 11ᵗʰ 1841
Died Oct. 6ᵗʰ 1851
Let us not murmur, God's own hand
Hath borne her from this wintry land
To one eternal Summer.

Talladega Cemetery

Malcolm McInnis
July 4, 1852
August 15, 1914
He stood
four square
to every wind
that blew.

Old Union Cemetery

In the vault beneath
rest the remains of

Mrs. Mary F. Wellborn

Consort of Dr. J. J. Wellborn
Born in Columbia Co. Ga.
on the 9th of Apr. 1922
And died in
Franklin, Macon Co. Ala.
on the 21th of May 1849

Lo, where this silent marble weeps,
A friend, a wife, a mother sleeps:
A heart within whose sacred cell
The peaceful virtues loved to dwell:
Affection warm and faith sincere
And soft humanity were there.

Magnolia Cemetery

Erected to the memory of
Dr. W. L. Hagood
who was born July 25 1825
and died January 1st 1864

Beyond the flight of Time,
Beyond the reign of Death,
There surely is some blessed shrine
Where Life is not a breath,
And Faith beholds the dying here
Translated to that happy sphere.

In that pure home of timeless joy,
Earth's parted friends shall meet
With smiles of Love that never fade
In Blessedness complete.
Where parting ne'er shall sink the heart,
Where Sorrow enters never,
But one with Jesus we shall dwell
And live with Him forever.

Unveil thy bosom, faithful Tomb,
Take these treasures to thy trust,
And give these sacred relics room
To slumber in the silent dust.

No pain, nor grief, nor anxious fear invades thy
bounds, no martial woes can reach the peaceful
sleeper here while angels watch the soft repose
by Jesus kept. God's dying son passed through
the grave and blessed the bed. Rest here,
Blest Spirit, till from His Throne, God shall
call thy spirit Home.

Possum Trot Cemetery

In Loving Memory of M. C. Williams
Born Oct. 4, 1848
Died May 11, 1902
What more appropriate could we
inscribe upon her tomb than our
dear Mother's dying words:
Lord, take me Home.

Providence Cemetery

J. E. Justice
June 30, 1831
Apr 15, 1901
Mighty unmasked
Reticent in nature
Dependable in character

We are so lonely
without you. Goodbye,
Father, but not forever.

Mt. Gilead Cemetery

John J. Walden
Born
Mar 1802
Died
Apr 1884
He shall
awake in the
Likeness
of God.

Hopewell
Cemetery

In Memory of
Nancy
Wife of P. Macon
Born 16 th Oct. 1798
Died 10th Sep. 1851
Sleep, Mother, Sleep Mother, we will
meet again.

Thou art gone, our precious darling,
Never more can thou return,
Thou must sleep a peaceful slumber
Till the Resurrection Morn.

Living, she was a joy and comfort
to her loved ones; dead, she is
another link in the golden chain
which links us to the heavenly
world.
Loachapoka Cemetery
Loachapoka, Alabama

George Culver
Apr 2 1837
July 24 1893
Let me die the death
of the Righteous,
and let my last end
be like His.
Troy City Cemetery

Elias Jenerett
Oct 24 1812
Oct 2 1852
Sweetly Sleeping.
Harrison Cemetery

Walter
Son of John S. and
Alcora Bennett
Born June 19   1881
Died Feb   21   1882
Tender Shepherd, thou hast stilled now,
Thy little lamb's brief weeping.
Ah, how peaceful, pale, and mild,
In it's narrow bed it's sleeping.
Opelika Cemetery

Here lie the Remains of
Elizabeth McFarland
Wife of R.F. McFarland
who was born in Jones Co. Ga.
May 15, 1815
and died in Macon Co. Ala.
Aug. 6, 1851
She left a Husband and five sons.
Having been a pious member of the Baptist
Church since 1835, she has left
Many friends to mourn her loss.
Tuskegee Cemetery

Sarah Wingard
Wife of
E.T. Crittenden

Dec. 22, 1849
June 9, 1931
In Memory of William
Wingard
This cemetery and church
donated by his granddaughter
Sarah Crittenden
1882 - 1883
Shady Grove Cemetery

Ena Mae Walker
born Nov. 17, 1901
died Nov. 18, 1922

Dearest love one
Thou have left us
The thy loss we
Deerly Feel
But tis God that
Has bereaved us
He can all our
Sorrow Heel.

Camp Ground Cemetery

Sacred to the memory of

Solomon Siler

A native of Chatham Co. N.C. who
was born April 22, 1788, and died
in Orion, Alabama, January 23, 1854
in his 66th yr

Thou art gone to the grave,
We no longer behold thee,
Nor tread the rough path of the world
By thy side.
God gave thee, He took thee, He mercifully
Enfolds thee. Death had not a sting, for
Thy Saviour had died.

In him were exemplified those virtues
which characterize a good citizen, a kind
father, and an affectionate companion.
Though the dust has returned to the
earth as it was, and the spirit unto God
Who gave it, yet the fond recollection of
an endeared and cherished

Husband

is indelibly enstamped on the imperishable
memory of a bereaved wife.

Orion Baptist Church Cemetery
Orion, Ala.

Elmira Caroline Crenshaw

The daughter of J.L. and Agnes Womack.
She married F.W. Crenshaw
Dec. 19, 1850, with whom she lived
in bonds of love until her death
which happened Nov. 3, 1861.

She professed the Christian religion and was a
member of the Methodist Protestant Church. She
was a dutiful daughter, an affectionate wife, a
kind mother, and a pious Christian. Retaining the
faculties of her mind to the last but strengthened
with the conscience of a blameless life and the
assurance of immortality beyond the grave through
faith in Christ, forgiving all and asking the forgiveness
of all if any were offended with her. Resigned
to her fate, she fearlessly met death, regretting
only the separation from her beloved husband and
children. And as a small tribute to departed worth
and as a testimonial of his love and duty and
that her memory may still live fresh and green
in the hearts of all, and more especially of her
children that she loved so well, this monument
is erected over her grave by her
bereaved Husband.

Crenshaw Family Cemetery
Butler County, Alabama

In Memory of
Elmira Caroline Crenshaw

Sweet Caroline, waking as in sleep,
Thou art but now a lovely dream,
A star that trembled o'er the deep,
Then turned from earth its tender beam.
But he who through life's dreary way
Must pass when heaven is veiled in wrath
Will long lament the vanished ray
That scattered gladness o'er his path.
Bright be the place of thy soul,
    No lovelier soul than thine
    Ere burst from its mortal control
    In the orbs of the blessed to shine
As thy soul shall immortally be
And our sorrows cease to repine
When we know God is with thee.
Light be the turf of thy tomb,
    May its verdure like emeralds be,
    There should not be a shadow of gloom
    In aught that reminds us of thee.
    Young flowers and an evergreen tree
May spring from the spot of thy rest
But nor cypress nor yew let us see
For why should we mourn for the blest?

Here sleeps the itinerant's wife
Mrs. M. E. Johnston
Consort of Rev. M. E. Johnston
of the North Ala. Conference
Born June 21, 1868   and
Died October 21, 1889

Camp Hill Cemetery
Camp Hill, Alabama

Simon R. May
Born
Sep. 10, 1819
Died
Feb. 8, 1819

He that giveth to the
poor, lendeth to
the Lord.
Gone but not forgotten.

Helicon Cemetery
Crenshaw Co.
Alabama

Julian Newton
Died
Feb 22 1893

Our darling one
Has gone before,
To greet us
on that
Beautiful
Shore.

Mt. Carmel Cemetery

To the Sacred
Memory of
W. P. Berry
Born
July 3 1822
Died
Dec 18 1895

He was Beloved
by God and man.
Aberfoil Cemetery

Little Isaac Brents
Tucker
Born
May 11 1902
Died
Sep 13 1903

Darling,
we miss thee.
Fairview Cemetery

In Memory of Clara Ethel
Dau. of C. C. and L. I. Jones
Born July 15 1879
Died July 23 1893
The golden gates opened and
a gentle voice said – Come.
And angels from the other
side welcomed our loved one
Home. Damascus Baptist
Church Cemetery

Mrs. Catherine Davis
Born May 29, 1860
Died July 1, 1895
Here lies one who in this life
Was a kind mother and a true wife
She was by many virtues blest
And piety among the best.

Shady Grove Cemetery

Sarah Sewell
Born 1826
Died Jan. 6, 1901
A link that
binds us to
Heaven.

Pliny O.
Woodham
Oct. 31, 1909
Mar. 6, 1929
May he
rest
in peace.

Mt. Carmel
Cemetery

Laura Jane
Dau. of
A. N. and E. F.
Born
Jan. 5, 1905
Died
Mar. 2, 1909

The little feet
in the golden street
Shall never go astray.

Friendship Baptist
Church Cemetery
Bullock Co., Ala.

A. H. Lovett
Dec. 5, 1835
Aug. 19, 1918
Enlisted U.S. Army
Capt. John Lamax
Co Mist Regiment
Ala Calvary
Dec. 1, 1863
Discharged
July 13, 1865
His toils are past,
His work is done,
He fought the fight,
The victory won.
Liberty Grove Cemetery

Maude Elenor
Dau. of
William and Marella
Gray
Nov 18 1899
May 26 1901
Waiting and watching
at the Beautiful Gate.
Baby Maude
Dadeville Cemetery

Sarah Vining
Henderson
Born 1911
Died 1912
Dear little hands,
I miss them so,
All through the night,
Wherever I go,
All through the night,
How lonely it seems,
For no little hands
Wake me out of my dreams.

Oakwood Cemetery

Ellen Hudgens
Born
Oct. 27, 1840
Died
July 25, 1907
She has entered
the Pearly Gate.
Antioch Primitive
Baptist Church
Cemetery

Cecil
Son of
J.J. and Lela
Nelson
Sep 1 1909
Sep 19 1917
Christ loved him
and took him home.
Friendship Baptist
Church Cemetery

In Memory of
Mrs. E.Y. McMorries
Born Sep. 10, 1851
Died at 7:30 P.M.
July 8, 1881
The pious Christian, the dutiful daughter,
the fond mother, the devoted wife,
rest here. In. Pace. Quiescat.
Rocky Mount
Cemetery
Crenshaw County

This Tablet Sacred To The Memory Of

Rev. Seymore B. Sawyer

Late pastor of the Methodist
Epispocal Church at Wetumpka
who resigned this life
24th September 1844
in the 36th year of his age
and the 13th of his ministry

Brother Sawyer was a plain, practical,
common-sense man who turned everything
to best account. Deeply pious, devoted to
his calling and eminently useful wherever
he labored. He was a man of one business,
a man of Christ.

How beauteous are their feet
Who stand on Zion's hill
And bring salvation on their tongues
And words of peace reveal.

Wetumpka Cemetery
Wetumpka, Alabama

Sacred to the memory of
Fitzgerald Byrd, M.D.

He was born near the Shoals of Oglethorpe,
in Warren Co. Ga. on the 7th of December
A.D. 1800. He died at Ft. Hull, Ala. on
the third of April, A.D. 1833.

These remains were removed to
this spot from their original place
of Sepulture at Fort Hull on the
7th of August, A.D. 1842.

His brave Sisters have erected
this monument to the memory of
their Beloved Brother.
A testimony of their Sincere
affection for him while living
and their deep grief
for his untimely and melancholy
Fate.
                    Wetumpka Cemetery
                    Wetumpka, Alabama

Sara F. Williamson
May 31 1840
May 1 1874
Come ye Blessed
She was a tender mother here
And in her life the Lord did fear.
Camp Ground Cemetery

J.J. Jordan
Mar. 18 1859
Oct. 4 1892
He was faithful to every
Duty — Thy trials ended,
Thy rest is won.
Banks

John Calhoun Black
Alabama
Pvt. Co. K   17   Regt. Ala. Inf
Confederate
States Army
Sep   9   1849
May   14   1927

Mary Susan	Parrilee M.
Wife of	Wife of
J. C. Black	J. C. Black
Born	Born
Mar 26 1849	Dec 20 1852
Died	Died
Feb 22 1896	May 4 1925
Gone Home	Gone Home

Damascus Baptist
Church Cemetery

Sacred to the memory of
Mary C. Easley
Born June 17, 1837
Departed this life
November 24, 1868

There is weeping on earth for the lost,
There is bowing in grief to the ground
But rejoicing and praise to the sanctified host
For a spirit in Paradise found.
Though brightness hath passed from the earth
Yet a star is newborn in the sky
And the soul hath gone to the land of its birth
Where are pleasures and fullness of joy.

And a new harp is strung
And a new song is given
To the breezes that float
Over the gardens of Heaven.

Opelika Cemetery
Opelika, Alabama

My Beloved Husband
T. M. Chance
Born   Mar 19 1847
Died   July 24 1911

He that followeth after
Righteousness and Mercy
findeth life, riches, and
Honor.   Wright's Chapel
                Cemetery

Marthe E.
Wife of
W.G. Mixson
Born
Sep 18 1846
Died
Jan 10 1902
Lord, she was Thine,
and not my own.
Thou hast done me
No wrong.
Miller's Tabernacle Cemetery

George Pittman
Born
Nov 1 1829
Died
Oct 21 1899

Peace be his ashes
In the grave,
Perfect his soul in
Heaven.
Weed Church Cemetery

Sacred to the memory of
Thomas Merriwether Barnett
who was born in Georgia
December 17, 1758
and died at Tallassee, Ala.
September 17, 1857

Whose usefulness and good example
will not end with his life.

Margaret Hawkins
Consort of
Thomas M. Barnett
Her gentle spirit took its flight after
long life's patient suffering
November 13, 1857
Aged 70 years
Blessed are the pure in spirit,
for they shall see God.

Martha Ellen
Daughter of
Thomas M. and Clara E. Barnett
who departed this life
after a short illness
August 12, 1858
aged 7 years and 6 months

Her spirit so gifted and pure
Has sought a brighter home,
But what was mortal of our
Darling Nellie sleeps here.

Our Darling Baby
Tucy
Daughter of
Thomas M. and Clara Barnett
who departed this life
October 25, 1859
Aged 11 months
Yesterday— with us,
Today— with the angels.

Rose Hill Cemetery
Tallassee, Alabama

This Tablet
Erected to the Memory of
Lucy Ann
Wife of Benjamin Micou
Only Daughter of Margaret H.
and Thomas M. Barnett,
After a lingering and most painful
illness of forty-five days
She departed this life
Sep. 28th, 1856

She leaves a husband, her little girls, Clara
and Lucy, and many friends to mourn the
loss of a wife, mother, and friend. Well
did she perform her part in life. She was
all a daughter, wife, and mother should be.
May her gentle Spirit
Rest in Peace.
By her side rest her two little angels
that never knew this world.

Rose Hill Cemetery
Tallassee, Alabama

In Memory of Evalin Vivian
Inf. Dau. of Chas. L. and M.E. Evans
Born Feb 4 1889
Died Aug 1 1890

Sweet Babe, tis hard to give thee up,
But God has willed we must.
Fond, aching hearts submit.
Hill's Chapel Cemetery

Kate McKenzie The Wife of
L.B. Carpenter was born Nov 30
1879 Died Jan. 25, 1952.
Preshers Memerey
Glorey to God.
Lizabeth Cemetery

George C. Crook
1908-1933
The sweet remembrances
of the just
Shall flourish when they
Sleep in dust.

Greenlawn Cemetery

Amanda Daughtery
October 13 1864
November 8 1933
She is calling us
all to Heaven.

Antioch West Cemetery

Sacred to the memory of
Mary William Scott
Dau. of William and Mary A.
Bibb and wife of Albert. U.
Scott who was born on the
8th of March 1809 and died
on the 9th of January 1837
in the 28 yr of her age.

Suddenly cut off in the midst of youth,
of beauty, and of hope, the tender relations
of daughter, sister, wife and mother
severed at a blow, she closed a life of
virtue by a death of peace. The Christian
faith she confessed and which she
adorned by her life, sustained her to
her death, soothing her last days and
consoling and guiding her with its
hopes . . .
Bibb Cemetery

Nathanel Edward Pennington
Born in York Dist. S.C.
June 30 1830
And was killed at the
Battle of Jonesboro, Ga.
September 1 1864
Tis pleasant to die for one's country.
Wetumpka Cemetery

Thomas Hightower
1851 – 1883

Stand still, ye rolling wheels and tyres,
Behold what ye have crushed.
All nature at the sight is hushed,
It was a thing – a man sublime.

Home is sadly changed, for thou art not there,
Angels have taken thee out of our care.
Dark is thy room and vacant thy chair
For thou art gone to that home so peaceful and fair
Gone and the seasons that come and go
And wreathe the grave in blossom and snow,
Snow on the bosom that sheltered us so
Gives anguish that none but an orphan can know.

Thy faithful hand thou'lt raise no more
To meet my loving fond caress,
For death's cold hand in passing o'er
Has snatched thee from affectionate breast.
What to me is life without thee?
Darkness and despair alone.
When with sighs I seek to find thee,
This tomb proclaims that thou art gone.

Westview Cemetery
La Fayette, Alabama

Patty Nuell

March 16, 1881

August 5, 1966

Wife of Henry Oliver Garrett

1904 - 1931

Wife of Omar Erskine Burns

1936 - 1966

Rosemundi

Rosespiritus.

Dadeville Cemetery

FOR FURTHER STUDY

GRAVESTONE WRITING AS FOLK LITERATURE

Gravestone writing as folk literature has received little scholarly attention, but there are several major studies of Anglo-American memorial art and numerous popular collections of epitaphs. An important early anthology was issued by John R. Kippax in 1877, *Churchyard Literature, A Choice Collection of American Epitaphs* (Chicago: S. C. Griggs and Company. Reps. Detroit: Singing Tree Press, 1969; Williamstown, Massachusetts: Corner House Publishers, 1978). Kippax established general classifications of epitaphs as admonitory, devotional, laudatory, professional, ludicrous, punning, satirical, and those written for eminent personages. In 1901 appeared W. H. Howe's *Here Lies: Being a Collection of Ancient and Queer Inscriptions from Tombstones* (New Amsterdam, New York: New Amsterdam Book Company) which, as the title indicates, features the odd, comic, and morbid. The specimens, chiefly English and evidently gathered from both gravestones and printed sources, include eulogies, literary memorials, anagrams, acrostics, and witticisms, as well as accounts of odd deaths.

A quarter of a century later W. H. Beable extended the tradition of oddity in *Epitaphs: Graveyard Humor and Eulogy* (New York: Thomas Y. Crowell, 1925. Reprinted, Detroit: Singing Tree Press, 1971). The extensive collection, "drawn freely from published examples . . . from old books, magazines, and periodicals, and from graveyards and other sources . . ." presents epitaphs for piemakers, auctioneers, brickmakers, parsons, shoemakers, actors, parish clerks, seamstresses, wandering ballad makers, doctors, lawyers, brewers, butchers, blacksmiths, apothecaries, cooks, midwives, clockmakers, and the famous; the introductory essay offers useful comments on the epitaph as historical document.

An invaluable nineteenth century guide to the early gravestones of America is Timothy Alden's *A Collection of American Epitaphs and Inscriptions with Occasional Notes* (New York: St. Marks Printer, 1814. Reprinted, New York: Arno Press, 1977, two volumes, originally published as five). Though gathered principally in Massachusetts, the collection contains representative epitaphs from New Hampshire, Rhode Island, Connecticut, New York, Pennsylvania, New Jersey, Virginia, Georgia, and Ohio; contemporary documents, newspaper accounts of deaths, murders, and crimes, published eulogies, and personal letters provide both folk and historical contexts. *American Epitaphs: Grave and Humorous* (New York: Dover Publications, Inc., 1973, first published under *Stories on*

Stone, New York: Oxford University Press, 1954) by Charles Wallis is a national treasury which contains "more than 750 epitaphs representing each decade in American history and all sections of the country," arranged according to subject and theme, together with some graveyard lore, anecdotes, tales, and contemporary accounts. From Alabama are cited the marker erected to Lincoln's assassin by Pink Parker in his front yard in Troy, the Clayton whiskey bottle tombstone, the comic Creama Tarter epitaph from Harrogate cemetery in Wetumpka, and the epitaph to a child buried in Marion, "Our Darling Billy Sugar." In the Foreword the author classifies epitaphs as folk literature and mentions three printed sources on which English and American carvers and epitaph composers might have drawn: John Bowden's *The Epitaph Writer* (London, 1791), *The Churchyard Lyrist* by George Mogride (London, 1833), and *The Silver Stole*, an American collection gathered by J. W. Cummings (New York, 1859).

A small but impressive volume is *Over Their Dead Bodies: Yankee Epitaphs and History* by Thomas C. Mann and Janet Greene (Brattleboro, Vermont: The Stephen Greene Press, 1962) with impressionistic sketches by George Daly; the presentation is chronological, and the selections from Connecticut, Massachusetts, and Vermont are nicely varied. A more objective approach is taken by the historian James Truslow Adams in *Memorials of Old Bridgehampton* (Long Island, New York: Ira J. Friedman, Inc. 1916. Reprinted

Fig. 60: The dove, carved within a recessed medallion, is an icon of Baptism and rebirth, of the Holy Spirit, and, when bearing the olive branch, of a New Heaven and a New Earth; the border is carved as linked fleurs-des-lis, the lilies of the field and those of royalty.

1962, Empire State Historical Publication XIII). Adams presents inventories of Mecox, Sagg, Poxabogue, Hayground, and Main Street cemeteries, c. 1733-1908. Interestingly, these cemeteries contain more gravestones without epitaphs than with them.

Studies in English memorial literature appeared as early as 1631 with the printing of John Weever's *Ancient Funerall Monuments* (available in exact reprint from the series The English Experience, No. 961, Norwood, New Jersey: Theatrum Orbis Terrarum, Ltd., 1979. Edited by Walter J. Johnson).

GRAVESTONES AS ARCHITECTURE/SCULPTURE

Katherine A. Esdaile's *English Church Monuments, 1510 to 1840* (New York: Oxford University Press, 1946) offers personable comment on memorial architecture and sculpture, the subsidiary arts of heraldry, carving, and costume, the makers of memorials, and the trade of stonemasonry. The introduction by Sacheverell Sitwell is a charmingly written overview of the subject, and the many photographs illustrate the evolution of memorial styles over three hundred years. Only a few last pages are devoted to the epitaph, but the author's claim that the epitaph of James Ramsey of Melrose (1751, from Ravenshaw's collection) is "one of the most impressive epitaphs in existence" is noteworthy, and the passage is well worth recalling here:

> The earthe goeth on the earthe
> Glistening like gold,
> The earthe goeth to the earthe
> Sooner than it wolde,
> The earthe builds on the earthe
> Castles and Towers,
> The earthe says to the earthe
> All shall be ours.

The definitive study of incised slabs is *Incised Effigial Slabs* by F. A. Greenhill (London: Faber and Faber, Ltd., 1976); volume one offers exhaustive comment on incised effigies, principally English brass and stone, as well as remarks on costumes and fashion, armorial bearings, heraldic devices, and inscriptions, with photographs; volume two indexes incised slabs in England, Germany, France, Holland, and Italy. English Christian monuments of the nineteenth century are well represented in *Church Monuments in Romantic England* by Nicholas Penny (The Paul Mellon Centre for Studies in British Art, New Haven and London: Yale University Press, 1977), and an American companion is *Victorian Cemetery Art* by Edmund V. Gillon, Jr. (New York: Dover Publications, Inc., 1972) with 260 photographs from Woodlawn Cemetery (the Bronx), Greenwood

(Brooklyn), Cambridge (New York), Laurel Hill (Philadelphia), Swan Point (Providence, Rhode Island), Mount Auburn (Cambridge, Massachusetts) and Lowell (Massachusetts).

Most commendable is the work of Britisher Frederick Burgess, *English Churchyard Memorials* (London: Lutterworth Press, 1963). Drawing on field research conducted throughout Great Britain, Burgess traces the evolution of typical monuments in every historical epoch, explores sources of symbolism and imagery, comments at length on lettering, inscriptions, and epitaphs, and offers a detailed account of gravestone masonry as a skilled trade. A comparable comprehensive study is much needed for America.

Field studies in epitaphs, emblems, and burial carvings are reported sporadically in various scholarly journals, and Duncan Emrich gives a section to the epitaph in his anthology *Folklore on the American Land* (Boston: Little, Brown and Company, 1972). Only lately, however, have scholars begun to assess the folk aspect of American memorial art, though gravestone carving was from the beginning a vernacular tradition passed from master to apprentice and journeyman, most often within the same family.

It was Harriette Merrifield Forbes who first understood the significance of the stonecutter. Her *Gravestones of Early New England: and the Men Who Made Them, 1653-1800* (Boston: Houghton Mifflin, 1927. Reprinted as volume 4 in the Da Capo Press Series in Architecture and Decorative Art, general editor, Adolf K. Placzek, New York: Da Capo Press, 1967) is a painstaking, meticulously documented study of styles and iconography as well as a carefully researched history of eighteenth century American stone cutters—the Lawsons of Charlestown, the Fosters of Dorchester, the Stone Cutter of Boston, William Park of Groton, the Thistle Carver of Tantuck, the Soules of Plympton, the Stevens family of Newport, Rhode Island. Her composite portrait of the stonecutter shows that he was influenced by other Colonial crafts, furniture, household utensils, and printing. Citings from journals, daybooks, and manuals of design and epitaphs kept by carvers like John Stevens and Joshua Hempsted suggest that Puritan gravestone art was rooted in a vast storehouse of folk symbols and visual expressions from folk life, literature, and thought.

Four decades later Harriette Forbes's successor, Allan I. Ludwig, completed her inquiry and issued *Graven Images: New England Stonecarving and Its Symbols, 1650-1815* (Middleton, Connecticut: Wesleyan University Press, 1966, with photographs). The first part analyzes the theological bases of Puritan gravestone symbolism and imagery and of burial rituals; the second closely examines the iconography of Puritan gravestone carvings; and the third expands and refines the Forbes's pioneer research in those contemporary documents pertaining to the folk practitioners of stone cutting. Throughout, the author addresses the reconciliation of the carved stone icons with the New England Puritan theological posture. His comparison of the vernacular and cultivated traditions concludes: "I suspect that we will find the New England rural stone carver participating in a universal pattern of form-making present in all early art and distinguished only by the eccentricities of individual hands" (p. 426). The Forbes collection consists of approximately 1,300 five-inch by seven-inch glass negatives deposited with the American Antiquarian Society. Ludwig's *Catalog of New England Stonecarving* indexes 4,000 photographs (Bolligen and Colonial Arts Foundation, copies filed with the Library of Congress). Though neither Forbes nor Ludwig considers the epitaph *per se* as folk literature, their studies point in that direction.

A decade after Ludwig's published studies, Peter Benes continued the exploration of Puritan memorial art in *The Masks of Orthodoxy: Folk Gravestone Carving in Plymouth County, Massachusetts, 1689-1805*, based on his examination of over 4,000 individual stones found mainly in Plymouth County. Founder and co-director of the Dublin Seminar for New England Folklife and co-founder of the Association for Gravestone Studies, the author had access to the glass negatives and the few remaining papers of Harriette Forbes (evidently she destroyed many of her notes) and to the unpublished findings of Dr. Ernest Caulfield, a pediatrician who issued twelve papers in the Connecticut Historical Bulletin, 1951–1967. Carefully assessing contemporary records in probate and other civil and religious records, Benes identifies twelve previously unknown stone carvers, emphasizes the ecclesiastical and theological background, especially the Half Way Covenant, the quarrel between the New Light and the Old Light which arose with the Great Awakening, and argues that Puritan gravestone carving is a "manifestly naive" folk art in which skull images or "spirit faces" symbolic of ghosts and spirits released by death were used deliberately as icons of Christian faith and doctrine.

Benes has also edited the essays and proceedings of the 1978 joint meetings of the Dublin Seminar for New England Folklife and the Association of Gravestone Studies, *Puritan Gravestone Art II*, (Boston: Boston University Press, 1979). Among these papers, Lance R. Mayer discusses the differences between "high" style and "plebian" or folk, with particular attention to pinwheels, rosettes, and hearts as folk motifs in gravestone and domestic arts; and Davis D. Hall and Allan I. Ludwig conceive of a nineteenth century Christian-folk culture in which an overriding figurative complex, perhaps derived from emblem books, unifies hymns, gravestone verses, music, iconography, and carved visual symbols.

Additionally, Dickran and Ann Tashjian have authored a study of Puritan memorial art, *Children of Change: The Art of Early New England Stonecarving* (Boston: Boston University Press, 1974), which scrutinizes Puritan folk artists and their monumental carvings and interprets the iconography and zeitgeist. A pleasant supplement to the Forbes, Ludwig, Benes, and Tashjian volumes is *Early American Gravestone Art in Photographs* by Francis Y. Duval and Ivan B. Rigby (New York: Dover Publications, Inc., 1979), and James Deetz includes a chapter on gravestones and epitaphs as folk artifacts and folk literature in his volume *In Small Things Forgotten: The Archeology of Early American Life* (Garden City, New York: Anchor-Doubleday paperback, 1977).

LOCAL SOURCES

Local antiquarian and historical efforts, well established by the early twentieth century on the Eastern seaboard, now surge throughout America. The cemetery census is a helpful guide to the historian, but alas, not always for the folklorist since the epitaph and notes on monument styles and iconography are often omitted. In Alabama, Archivist Peter Brannon spearheaded cemetery census research in Montgomery County, and there are several manuscripts deposited in the Alabama Archives by numerous individuals and volunteer agencies, a few of which include transcriptions of epitaphs. Some historical associations have undertaken complete inventories of every known cemetery within the county, for example, that of Pike County (*Alabama Historical Quarterly*, vol. 35, 1973), which, unfortunately, omits epitaphs. Now and then a master's thesis is devoted to cemetery surveys. Auburn University's Ralph Draughon Library has on file Nella Chambers's "A Survey of the Older Cemeteries of Chambers County" (1954) and a two-volume *Cemeteries of Madison County by Dorothy Scott Johnson* (Huntsville, Alabama: Johnson Historical Publications, 1971).

　　The standard for local cemetery investigation has been set by *A History of Church Street Graveyard: Mobile, Alabama*. Containing a complete inventory, together with notes on monument styles and emblems and an introductory essay which identifies historical personages, it was compiled by Col. and Mrs. Soren Nelson under the auspices of the Historic Mobile Preservation Society (Mobile, Alabama: Jordan Printing Company, 1963. Rep. Mobile, Alabama: Southern Lithographing Company, 1974). Recently, John S. Sledge has written *Cities of Silence: A Guide to Mobile Historic Cemeteries* (Tuscaloosa: University of Alabama Press, 2002), a very fine study, with photos by Sheila Hagler.

　　Another local collection of national importance is *Bruton Parish Churchyard: A Guide to the Tombstones, Monuments, and Mural Tablets* published by Bruton Parish Church of Williamsburg, Virginia, 1976, an American Bicentennial Project spearheaded by the women of Bruton Church and a communal effort by members of the parish. Energetic local research efforts throughout America could lead to systematic collection and storage in central depositories, state archives and university libraries, and, ultimately, to an index of American folk epitaphs.

THE HISTORY OF WRITING

The epitaph as inscription should be studied within the context of the history of all language, from origins in pictograms, syllabaries, hieroglyphs, and alphabets on permanent and semipermanent surfaces to evolution as handwriting on vellum, parchment, papyrus, and paper, thence to movable type and press, and finally to the present computer logogram replicated by photographic and laser printing. Over 3,000 languages, excluding

Fig. 61: Twin columns linked by a rose garland and draped urns commemorate the life, death, love, and marriage of James and Eliza.

thousands of dialects, are now in use. The stunning achievements of researchers in the discovery and analysis of evidence and the systematic formulation of linguistic theory commenced with the finding of the Rosetta Stone in 1799 by Napoleon's soldiers and the decipherment of parallel texts in Greek and in hieroglyphic and demotic Egyptian. For the next one hundred years the Mediterranean Basin revealed its riches in language.

Our century has seen only one important analyst of the evolution of print, Stanley Morison, who spent his entire life in the quest for a perfect mass production type. Arduously researching calligraphic and type models, he became an historian of the alphabet, inscriptions, writing, and type design, and prophesied the photographic computer printer. For the Monotone Corporation, Morison cut his famous Bembo as well as an italic and a roman based on Garamond. His collaboration with Eric Gill, English sculptor and letter designer, reinforced his concept of type as sculpture and together they created the Gill Sans, a type based on Gill's sculptured block letters for signs. Morison's triumph was the *London Times* roman, a face which paid tribute to the heritage of calligraphic script, yet was adapted fully to newspaper legibility.

Eric Gill is the only major twentieth-century artist who left a significant body of monuments and monumental inscriptions. He began as a carver of tombstones and trained first under Edward Johnson, whose *Writing and Illuminating and Lettering* (New York, Taplinger, 1977) ranks as probably the most influential study of calligraphy in this century. In addition to the Gill Sans, the Perpetua, the Golden Cockerel, and the Joanna type fonts, Gill designed war memorials throughout England, had a long career in public lettering and monumental carvings, and executed tombs for Rupert Brooke, Aubrey Beardsley, and G. K. Chesterton. Malcolm Yorke has recently issued the admirable study *Eric Gill: Man of Flesh and Spirit* (New York: Universe Books, 1982, with photographs). Only the final chapter, however, considers Gill's work in type design.

Gill's own assessment of his life and art appears on his memorial: Stone Carver. That he identified himself as a folk artisan is more than a matter of idle interest, and one cannot help remembering Jude Hawley in Thomas Hardy's novel *Jude the Obscure*. A country lad at Marygreen, Jude apprentices himself to a stonemason and learns to cut inscriptions and repair church masonry; but his heart is set on scholarship and his craft is only a means of reaching Christminster (Oxford) which looms in his imagination as the New Jerusalem of all learning and beauty; his tragic quest for knowledge and his tormented love for the "new woman" Sue Bridehead are both doomed, and near his deathbed are his precious volumes of Virgil, Horace, and the Greek New Testament, tinged with stone dust. On Jude's first night at fabled Christminster he falls asleep under the spell of the spectres of brilliant men associated with the university. Among the passages Hardy chose for Jude's reveries was this from Joseph Addison's *Spectator 26*:

When I look upon the tombs of the great, every motion of envy dies in me; when I read the epitaphs of the beautiful, every inordinate desire goes out; when I meet with the grief of parents upon a tombstone, my heart melts with compassion; when I see the tombs of the parents themselves, I consider the vanity of grieving for those whom we must quickly follow.*

That Morison was a lifelong scholar of monumental inscriptions who revolutionized the most important newspaper of the English speaking world, that Gill was an artist in both monumental carving and type design, that Jude Fawley the stone mason longed for the knowledge hidden in printed words—these are not accidents. The historical relationship of writing, printing, book production, and inscriptional memorial art is a study which holds possibilities for understanding how the human brain invents, learns, and stores language as expressive and pragmatic communication. Correspondences in the lettering, decorative borders, and ornamental motifs of title pages and gravestone carvings, 1750-1950, are often discoverable, and the lettering of memorials shows marked affinities with poster art and sign painting, folk crafts still vigorously practiced throughout rural and small town America. Ball parks and stadiums are blazoned with historic calligraphic styles, emblems, and signs which appear visually as hieroglyphs, syllabaries, and pictograms but serve as logos of the contemporary marketplace.**

Most studies of the history of writing and language are aimed at scholars. Elmer D. Johnson's *Communication: An Introduction to the History of Writings, Books, and Libraries* (New York: The Scarecrow Press, Inc., 1966) is a guide for the general reader, and *A Study of Writing* by I. J. Gelb (Chicago: The University of Chicago Press, 1952) surveys world writing systems, including primitive pictography, descriptive-representational forms, Egyptian, Sumerian, Hittite, and Chinese writing, syllabaries and the Greek alphabet. Currently, there is much interest in Anglo-European runes. R. Elliott's *Runes* (Manchester: Manchester University Press, 1963) and *An Introduction to English Runes* by R. I. Page (London: Methuen, 1983) are recommended, and Ralph Blum's *The Book of Runes* (New York: St. Martin's Press, 1983) is popular with college students and general readers. Similarly, the art of calligraphy is enjoying a revival.

Manuals are widely available. For the specialist, there is *The Calligrapher's Handbook*, edited by C. M. Lamb (London: Faber and Faber, Ltd., MCMLVI, MCMLXVIII), with

---

*Thomas Hardy, *Jude the Obscure*, ed. by Norman Page, New York: W. W. Norton and Company, 1978, p. 67.

** *The Quarterly Journal of the Library of Congress*, no longer issued, has habitually included a wide range and numerous specimens of historic title pages, posters, lettering, type scripts, manuscript illumination, and book production styles; see 28:3, 1971, pp. 211-216, for reproductions of fifteenth and sixteenth century German, French, and Venetian acquisitions in the Rosenwald collection; also Renata Shaw's "Nineteenth Century Tobacco Label Art" (28:2, 1971, pp. 76-102); "Craftsman in a Machine Age," a study of the American type designer Frederick W. Goudy (34:2, 1977, pp. 97-115); and "The Library's Earliest Incunabula" by Roger J. Trienens (33:1, 1076, pp. 55-71).

essays on pigments, inks, paper, heraldry, book design and binding.

And the editors hope that *Gone Home* will stimulate collection of epitaphs, a pleasurable investigation well adapted for church, civic, garden, professional, literary, and historical organizations. Ideally, every town, church, and urban cemetery in Alabama should be inventoried, such survey to include the epitaph as well as notes on styles, carving, lettering, and iconography. Not much is required in the way of equipment—a reliable camera and portable tape recorder, pens and notebooks, a few rolls of butcher paper, sturdy pencils with thick leads for rubbings, which may be sprayed with fixative and framed. Amateur photographers will find challenges everywhere, local newspapers may wish to print collections, and historical organizations might fund publication. After a few visits to local cemeteries, the collector's sense of time and history will be stirred, his faith and hope in mankind refreshed, and his love for ordinary folk renewed.

Fig. 62: Olivia Solomon and son Will, right foreground, at Live Oak Cemetery in Selma, Alabama.

INDEX

The Solomon family about 1979 at the grave of folklorist Ruby Pickens Tartt, Livingston, Alabama. From left, Will, Olivia, Suzannah, Jack, and Jackie Solomon.

JACK and OLIVIA SOLOMON are well-known Alabama folklorists and writers. Their books include *Cracklin Bread and Asfidity, Zickary Zan, Ghosts and Goosebumps, Sweet Bunch of Daisies,* and *Honey in the Rock.* Mrs. Solomon is also the author of *Wild, Wildwood Flower and Other Deep South Tales* and *Five Folk Comedies.* Jack, born in Brantley, Alabama, grew up in Luverne, and Olivia was born in Tallassee, where they now live. They have three children—Jacqueline Harriette Ellen, Suzannah Olivia, and James Marion Willard. Jack received his A.B. at Troy State, M.A. at Columbia University, Ed.S. from George Peabody College, and completed postgraduate work at Auburn University. Olivia attended the University of Alabama, where she earned both the A.B. and the M.A. degrees.

    SUZANNAH SOLOMON is the daughter of Jack and Olivia. Her photographs in this volume were made on family field trips while she was a student at Tallassee High School. Suzannah is a graduate of New College, University of Alabama, and is the proprietor of Suzannah's Photography in Tallassee.